To Alan

Wishing you a complete and spe[...]

Best wishes fro[...] [...]5".

VESEY NORMAN

ARMS AND ARMOUR

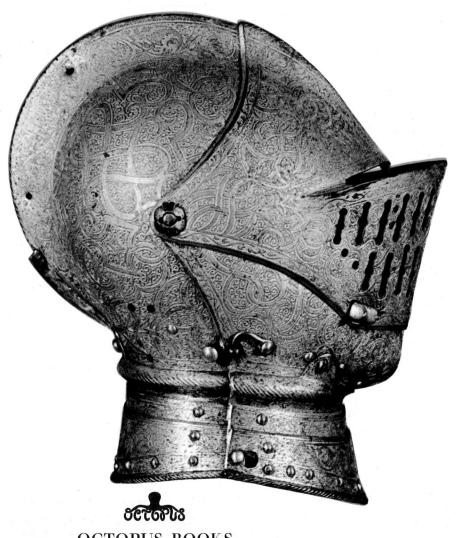

OCTOPUS BOOKS

Acknowledgments

The author would like to thank four friends most warmly for their support and advice in writing this book: Mr Claude Blair of the Victoria and Albert Museum, Dr Bruno Thomas and Dr Ortwin Gamber of the Kunsthistorisches Museum, Vienna, and Freiherr Alexander von Reitzenstein of the Bayerisches Nationalmuseum, Munich. He would like to express his gratitude to Mr E. T. Coelho for drawing his attention to the importance of the Pistoia altar-piece.

Figure 90 is reproduced by gracious permission of Her Majesty The Queen. The author and publishers wish to thank the following owners and collectors for permission to reproduce paintings and armour in their collections: the Marquess of Lothian, figure 73; Baron H. H. Thyssen-Bornemisza, figure 62; Hans Graf Trapp, figures 43, 45, 49, 51.

The following illustrations are reproduced by courtesy of the authorities, directors and curators of the following museums, art galleries, libraries and treasuries: Aachen Cathedral, figure 8; Angoulême Cathedral, figure 6; the Armouries, HM Tower of London, figures 71, 88, 92, 119; the Bayerisches Nationalmuseum, Munich, figures 31, 32, 46, 47, 54, 123, 125; the Bodleian Library, Oxford, figures 37–9; the British Museum, the endpapers, figures 15, 16, 27, 33, 118; Canterbury Cathedral, figure 36; Castel Sforza, Milan, figure 4; Christ Church, Oxford, figure 26; the Church of San Zeno Maggiore, Verona, figure 5; the Convent Church, Himmelkron, Bavaria, figure 30; Essen Cathedral, figure 97; the Fitzwilliam Museum, Cambridge, figure 121; the Gallerie dell'Accademia, Venice, figure 59; the Galleria Sabauda, Turin, figure 89; the Historisches Museum, Basel, figure 116; the Historisches Museum der Stadt Wien, figures 40, 48; the Kunsthistorisches Museum, Vienna, figures 50, 52, 55, 60, 61, 69, 72, 77, 83, 95, 102, 103, 105, 115; the London Museum, Kensington Palace, figures 98, 122; Magdeburg Cathedral, figure 11; the Metropolitan Museum of Art, New York, figures 24 (Cloisters Collection, Gift of John D. Rockefeller Jr, 1948), 68 (Rogers Fund, 1904), 84 (Munsey Fund, 1932), 108 (Rutherford Stuyvesant Collection, Gift of Alan Rutherford Stuyvesant, 1949); the Ministre d'Education de France, figure 34; the Musée de l'Armée, Paris, figure 64, the Musée du Louvre, Paris, figures 57, 85, 96; the Museo del Prado, Madrid, figure 65; the Museo Nazionale (Bargello), Florence, figure 76; the Museum für Deutsche Geschichte, Berlin, figure 10; the Národni Museum, Prague, figure 3; the National Historical Museum, Stockholm, figure 25; the Niedersächsische Landesgalerie, Hanover, figure 18; Pershore Abbey, Worcestershire, figure 13; the Pierpont Morgan Library, New York, figures 7, 21; the Pinacoteca di Brera, Milan, figure 58; Pistoia Cathedral, figures 19, 20; the Real Armeria, Madrid, figures 66, 67, 70, 75, 79, 81, 127; the Rijksmuseum, Amsterdam, figure 87; the Royal Scottish Museum, Edinburgh, figures 28, 99; the Schatzkammer der Residenz, Munich, figures 101, 107, 114; the Schweizerisches Landesmuseum, Zurich, figure 29; the Staatliche Kunstsammlung, Dresden, figures 80, 82, 86, 100; Stoke d'Abernon Church, Surrey, figures 12, 22; the Tiroler Landes-Museum Ferdinandeum, Innsbruck, figures 53, 93; the Tøjhusmuseet, Copenhagen, figure 104; Toledo Cathedral, figure 109; the Universitätsbibliothek, Heidelberg, figure 23; the Universitätsbibliothek, Tubingen (Depot der ehem Preuss. Staatsbibl.), figure 14; the Victoria and Albert Museum, London, figures 56, 94, 110, 117, 124; the Wallace Collection, London, the title page, figures 2, 78, 91, 106, 111, 112, 113, 120, 126, 128, 129; Wells Cathedral, figure 17; Winchester Cathedral, figure 1; the Württembergische Landesbibliothek, Stuttgart, figure 63.

The following illustrations were obtained from the following sources: Archives Photographiques, Paris, figure 6; the Bayerisches Nationalmuseum, figure 30; the Landesbildstelle, Württemberg, figure 41; the Mansell Collection, London, figures 35, 58; the Ministry of Public Buildings and Works, London, figures 66, 70, 127; the National Buildings Record, London, figure 17; the National Galleries of Scotland, Edinburgh, figure 73; the Soprintendenza della Belle Arti, Florence, figures 19, 20; The Times, London, figure 36; the Victoria and Albert Museum, figures 9, 12, 22, 42, 56.

Figures 35, 58 were photographed by Alinari; figure 8 by Ann Bredol-Lepper; figure 64 by Bulloz; figures 40, 48 by Lucca Chmel; figure 57 by Maurice Chuzeville; figures 110, 124 by A. C. Cooper; figures 126, 128 by Henry Dixon & Sons; figure 3 by Josef Ehm; figure 62 by Foto-Brunel; figure 97 by Foto-Witzel; figure 73 by Ideal Studio; figure 23 by Lossen-Foto; figures 43, 45, 49, 51 by Federico Arborio Mella; figures 52, 60, 77, 95, 103, 105 by Erwin Meyer; figure 90 by Photo Studios; figure 28 by Tom Scott; figure 1 by E. A. Sollars; figure 121 by Stearn & Sons; figures 71, 88, 91, 92, 120, 129 by Derrick Witty.

The drawing of the parts of an armour, figure 2, was made by Russell Robinson.

This edition first published 1972 by
OCTOPUS BOOKS LIMITED
59 Grosvenor Street, London W.1

ISBN 7064 0034 8

Preceding page
Close helmet, South German, *c.* 1560

PRODUCED BY MANDARIN PUBLISHERS LIMITED AND PRINTED IN HONG KONG

Contents

EXPLICIVNT CAPITVLA :

INCIPIT LIBER IOSVE BENNVN :

VT. POST. MORE MOYSI.

serui dñi. loqueret dñs ad iosue filium nun ministru

4

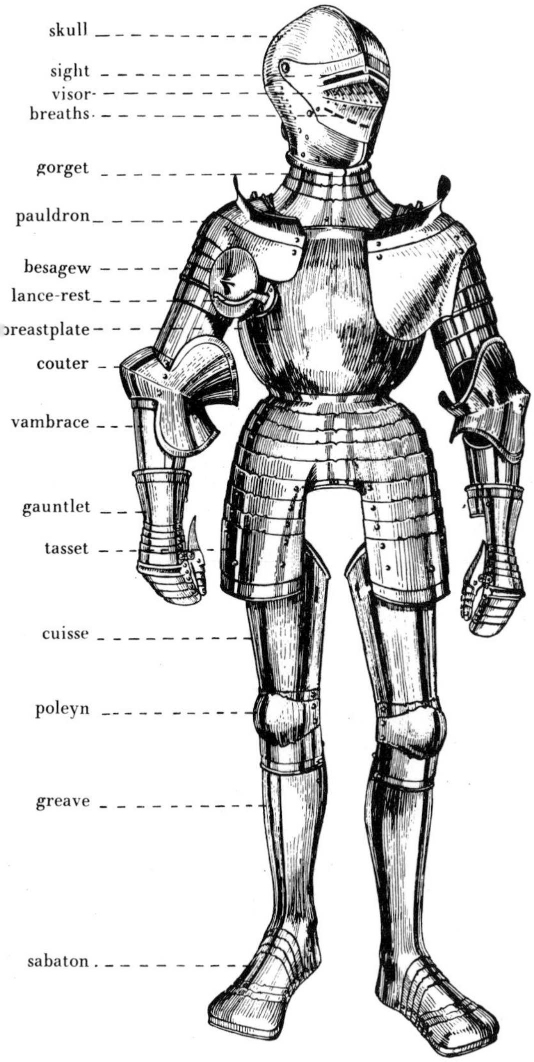

MAIL AND ITS DEVELOPMENT

skull
sight
visor
breaths
gorget
pauldron
besagew
lance-rest
breastplate
couter
vambrace
gauntlet
tasset
cuisse
poleyn
greave
sabaton

2 The parts of an armour

THROUGHOUT THE ELEVENTH and twelfth centuries fashions in armour were similar all over Western Europe. The armour of the Norman knights in the Bayeux Tapestry, probably English work before 1077, is very like that in a tapestry of *c.* 1180 from Baldishol Church, Norway, and that in a Spanish manuscript of the Commentaries on the Apocalypse by St Beatus, completed in 1109, now in the British Museum.

The armour consisted of a knee-length shirt of mail, that is of interlocking iron rings, with three-quarter sleeves, a conical helmet with a nasal, and a large kite-shaped shield. The mail shirt, called a hauberk, was split up the front and back almost to waist level so that it hung on either side of the saddle. It usually had a mail hood made in one piece with it, but the Bayeux Tapestry shows some hauberks terminated at the neck, and in a few cases the hood may have been of cloth or leather. This embroidery and one Spanish manuscript show a square outline on the breast but it is not clear whether this represents a mail reinforce, a flap closing the neck of the hauberk, or the attachment of a plate beneath the mail. Finds at Hjortspring and Thorsbjerg in Denmark prove that mail had been known in western Europe from at least the third century BC.

The helmet is probably derived from late Roman and Migration Period examples, specimens of which have been excavated at widely scattered sites in Europe. These consist of a brow-band supporting metal straps crossing over the skull, to which was fixed a lining of horn or metal. They usually have a short nasal and cheek-pieces, and have had a mail curtain at the back of the neck. The cheek-pieces seem to have disappeared early, although they still occur on the knights of several sets of Norse chessmen of the twelfth century in the British Museum, the helmets in some cases having a nape plate at the centre of the back [figure 15].

A few helmets of the tenth to twelfth centuries have survived. The finest example, and the earliest surviving piece of European armour which has not been excavated, is preserved in Prague Cathedral and is believed to have belonged

1 (*left*) The Joshua initial from the Winchester Bible, English, *c.* 1160–70; it shows very long surcoats, and mail sleeves leaving only the fingers uncovered

5

3 Helmet, traditionally of St Wenceslaus, who died in 935, preserved in the Treasury of Prague Cathedral

4 Warriors, one in scale armour, from the Porta Romana, Milan, late twelfth-century

to St Wenceslaus, who died in 935. It is a typical conical helmet of the period, the skull made in one piece, with a separate nasal and lower rim riveted on and inlaid with silver [figure 3].

In a few cases the Bayeux Tapestry shows what appears to be mail hosen or stockings but these did not come into general use until much later. It is not clear what was worn under mail at this time. The portion of the Bayeux Tapestry showing the dead being stripped, where they are seen to be naked under the mail, has been very heavily restored since the eighteenth century and is therefore unreliable. As late as the middle of the thirteenth century the Maciejowski Bible shows a mail shirt being put on over a simple tunic. One would expect mail worn in this way to cause acute discomfort to the wearer in a relatively short time.

At least one figure in the Tapestry shows a tunic-shaped garment possibly made of overlapping scales. There are earlier references to armour made of iron plates, and some has even been excavated from a ship-burial of the Vendel period at Valsgärde in Uppland, Sweden.

The long kite-shaped shield, concave towards the body and with rounded top, is the typical horseman's shield of the period, but many representations show a round shield used by the infantry and very occasionally by the cavalry. Both types frequently have bands radiating from the central boss and a broad edging, which may represent metal reinforces. Although the round shield from the seventh-century Saxon ship-burial at Sutton Hoo is only bound with gilt bronze, Giraldus Cambrensis refers to the round red shield of the Norsemen in Ireland 'strengthened with iron round about'. The main part of the shield was of wood covered with leather. The shield was held by passing the fore-arm either through a series of straps on the back or through a simple strap and gripping a bar set behind the hollow of the boss. A long loose strap allowed the shield to be hung up in the hall, or slung on the back when both hands were required in combat.

From the second quarter of the twelfth century the long shield was given a straight upper edge, presumably because this increased visibility. Typical knights of the early twelfth century are shown on the carved doorway of the Church of San Zeno Maggiore at Verona, c. 1139 [figure 5]. The long skirts of some form of under-tunic hang down to mid-calf from beneath the hauberk, and the points of the conical helmets are slightly tilted forward. In a few cases the back edge of the helmet is swept down slightly to protect the neck, as shown on a carving on the front of Angoulême Cathedral of c. 1128 [figure 6]. The hauberk usually had wrist-length sleeves and leg armour was becoming more common. In some cases this consisted of mail stockings braced up to the waist-belt; in others the mail only covered the front of the leg and was laced across the back.

By the end of the century the arms of the hauberk frequently terminated in mail bag-mittens which consisted of a bag for the fingers with another for the thumb. The palm was only covered by leather or fabric and was slit so that the hands could emerge when battle was not imminent. They were held tight round the wrist by means of a strap or thong.

During the second half of this century the skull of the nasal helmet was often rounded as in the Huntingfield Psalter (English, late twelfth century) and by about 1200 a cylindrical flat-topped version had been introduced. From c. 1180 a face-guard pierced with breaths and sights was added to the helmet which necessitated the use of identification signs from which the science of Heraldry developed. One of the Lewis chessmen is wearing a new style of helmet, the kettle-hat, a broad-brimmed, open-faced head-piece which was to remain in service as long as armour survived [figure 15].

Apart from mail, the main form of body armour of the twelfth century was scale. A hauberk complete with coif, both formed of small scales, is shown on the Porta Romana at Milan of the late twelfth century [figure 4]. The chronicler Wace in *Roman de Rou* (c. 1160–1174) frequently mentions the use of the gambeson, a body armour of quilted

5 Figure from the Church of San Zeno Maggiore at Verona, carved c. 1139 by Nicholaus and Wiligelmus

6 Figures from the front of Angoulême Cathedral, c. 1128, showing fluted helmets, one elongated backwards to guard the neck

material. Early mediaeval illustrations rarely make it clear what material is portrayed, but the Maciejowski Bible shows many apparently quilted tunics, some of them with sleeves.

During the latter half of the century, a loose flowing surcoat was adopted, perhaps in imitation of the Saracens, or possibly to protect the armour from the rain or to prevent it from overheating in the sun of the Holy Land. By the thirteenth century it was in almost universal wear, and, although most early representations are self-coloured, by the end of the century it had become the field for heraldic display. One of the earliest representations of the surcoat, in the Winchester Bible of about 1160 to 1170, shows surcoats sweeping the ground [figure 1], but normally they were worn to midcalf or shorter.

Throughout the thirteenth century continued attempts were made to improve the defensive qualities of armour. The silver shrine of Charlemagne in Aachen Cathedral, made between 1200 and 1207, shows flat-topped helms with face-guards and small neck defences [figure 8]. It also shows the padded arming cap worn under the coif. The west front of Wells Cathedral, Somerset, c. 1230 to 1240, includes representations of complete cylindrical flat-topped helms and the flat-topped coif designed to go under this form of helm. A helm of this type was excavated in Pomerania, and is now in the Museum für Deutsche Geschichte in Berlin [figure 10]. It has holes for the attachment of a lining. Literary sources indicate that the helm was laced on to the head. The coif frequently had a strap or thong threaded through the mail at brow level, which, as indicated on

7 A page from the Maciejowski Bible, French, c. 1250; the upper part shows an assault on a city

8 Part of the silver Shrine of Charlemagne in Aachen Cathedral, made between 1200 and 1207, showing helmets with face and neck guards

REGIS : HIC CECIVADERVN

9 Part of the Bayeux Tapestry, probably English work before 1077, which shows Norman cavalry attacking the English position

monumental effigies, was tied at the back. The ventail, the flap by which the neck of the coif was closed, was held up by this brow-strap, but in other cases it was tied or buckled to the side of the coif. Many knights wore a broad band round the coif immediately above the brow-strap, which literary references show to have been a jewelled circle.

The Wells figures also illustrate what is apparently an arming cap with a turban-like roll round the skull which would give the coif a flat top. Here and in the Temple Church, London, this type of cap is also shown worn over the mail presumably to support the flat-topped helm [figure 17]. One of the Temple effigies has a flat-topped head piece with open face and what appears to be a metal strap edging the face-opening. A number of French effigies which no longer survive appear to have shown a small vertical bar attached to the coif on each side of the face.

The hauberk was by now invariably only a little longer

9

10 Helm of the second half of the thirteenth century, excavated at Schlossberg bei Dargen Pomerania

than knee-length and had arms with bag-mittens attached. The hosen enclosed the whole legs and feet and a strap round the leg below the knee served to reduce the drag on the waist. The fact that at Bouvines in 1214 Reginald de Boulogne is said to have been saved from a thrust beneath the hauberk by his hosen being firmly attached to it, suggests that they were complete breeches.

The Wells statues show two kinds of surcoats: some are the normal loose-flowing garment, hanging in many folds; the shoulders of others are smooth and stand up clear of the wearer's shoulders. In one case this second type has a high stiff collar [figure 17]. These stiffer surcoats certainly suggest some sort of body defence worn over the mail but by the end of the century representations of more solid forms of body armour occur.

A close-fitting body defence opening down the sides can be seen at the armholes of the surcoats of two English sepulchral effigies of about 1280, the one in the Temple Church, London, traditionally of Gilbert Marshal, and the other at Pershore, Worcestershire, [figure 13]. These perhaps represent the *curie* or *paires de cuiraces* of contemporary documents. The name suggests that they were made of leather. A statue of St Maurice in Magdeburg Cathedral, dating from the second half of the century, shows a poncho-like garment from the front part of which broad flaps extend under the arms and buckle together down the centre of the back. The representation of rivet heads on the outside of this garment above the waist suggest that this part is lined with plates [figure 11]. The ordinary surcoat of about this time and continuing into the first half of the fourteenth century is also represented with vertical plates riveted to the inside of the material [figure 18]. This system probably developed into the garment known in the fourteenth century as *plates* or as a *pair of plates*. A few pieces of scale armour have been excavated at the castle of Montfort which fell to the Saracens and was destroyed in 1271.

Until the middle of the century the large kite-shaped shield remained in vogue, but already a smaller form, shaped like the base of a flat-iron, was becoming fashionable. Both types were usually slightly curved to the body. In Italy the kite-shaped shield remained in use by the infantry until the fifteenth century.

The Maciejowski Bible, which contains French miniatures of *c.* 1250, is a valuable source of information about this period [figures 7 and 21]. The majority of the knights

11 Figure of St Maurice in Magdeburg Cathedral, late thirteenth-century, showing an early form of the *pair of plates*

are still dressed exactly like the Wells figures. The nasal helmets worn by the Gentile knights are probably an early case of antiquarianism or the artist's attempt to show Saracen armour. In many cases, where the coif is thrown back, a close fitting, heavily quilted arming cap is shown, and in two cases a small steel cap; the latter, called a *cervellière* in contemporary inventories, is also frequently worn over the coif. This is the typical head-piece of the infantry who also These were flat rectangles, diamonds or circles attached to the points of the shoulders [figures 26 and 37]. Monumental effigies and paintings show that they were worn in such a way that the flat surface was visible to the bystander when the knight was viewed from the side. They were usually decorated heraldically, and contemporary inventories indicate that they were made of parchment or leather, and therefore they presumably had no defensive value. They continued to be worn until the 'forties of the following century.

Greaves are very occasionally illustrated during this century and are mentioned under the name of *jamberis* in a list of armour provided for Prince Edward of England and John of Lancaster *c.* 1299. An English Statute of Arms written before 1295 mentions *espaulers* or shoulder defences, and there are many late thirteenth-century references to gauntlets of whalebone or plate.

By the end of the century the helm frequently had a skull shaped like a hazel-nut, in order to produce a glancing surface to deflect a blow away from this most vulnerable place. The brass of Sir Roger de Trumpington, at Trumpington in Cambridgeshire, shows the helm attached by a chain to the waist-belt so that it should not be lost in action. The most popular form of crest of the period was fan-shaped, sometimes of painted parchment on a metal or wooden frame, sometimes of feathers. A similar crest was often fitted on the horse's head.

Horse-armours of mail are represented in the art of the

12 (*above*) Memorial brass of Sir John D'Aubernoun at Stoke d'Abernon, Surrey, English. 1277

13 English effigy of *c.* 1280 in Pershore Abbey, Worcestershire, showing the ventail open and some form of solid body armour

second half of the century and a number of Statutes of Arms mention 'covered horses', meaning horses covered with armour either of mail or of quilted fabric. The adoption of the surcoat by the knight was soon followed by the adoption of a cloth housing often decorated heraldically, and plate horse-armour was in use by the end of the century.

have a number of different forms of kettle-hat. One is made on the principle of an old-fashioned wooden bucket of hoop and stave construction, the other appears to consist of a broad brim and a broad, keeled band crossing the skull fore and aft, while the skull is formed by filling the gap between keel and brim with thinner plates. A number of helmets of this type have been excavated in Scandinavia.

The usual body armour of the infantry in the Maciejowski Bible appears to have been a sleeveless gambeson with

15 (*below*) Three of a group of twelfth-century Norse chessmen found at Uig in Lewis; the shield-biter is a berserk

16 Miniature by Mathew Paris, English, *c.* 1250 – notice the knight's unusual leg covering

17 Two knights on the west front of Wells Cathedral, English, *c.* 1230–40; the further figure shows an arming cap worn over the coif

18 Sleeping guard from a reliquary at Wienhausen, German, second half of the thirteenth century; he wears a reinforced surcoat

a wide stiff collar, perhaps lined with metal, worn either over a hauberk or over another gambeson with long sleeves sometimes terminating in bag or finger gloves [figure 7]. The only indication of any other form of body armour is a small stiff waistcoat of poncho form [figure 21].

The *Eneide* Manuscript of *c.* 1220 shows some sort of thigh defence worn over the mail hosen and in the mid-century drawings by Mathew Paris in the *Lives of the Offas* they are shown as if quilted. In the Maciejowski Bible one figure draws a pair of these gamboised cuisses onto his legs. Plate knee defences first appear in the Trinity College Apocalypse of *c.* 1230. From the third quarter of the century, these were often worn strapped over the thigh defences or attached to them. A Mathew Paris drawing in the British Museum shows some form of greave and shoe apparently covered with closely placed rings. Here, at least, it is clear that the mail hosen are not joined at the fork [figure 16]. An apparently unique thirteenth-century representation of small plates attached to the mail over the elbows appears on the effigy of William Longspée the Younger in Salisbury Cathedral, *c.* 1260.

By the beginning of the last quarter of the century, the coif was again made separate from the hauberk, which now ended above the knee, sometimes showing the lower edge of the quilted under-tunic or aketon. The sleeves of the hauberk now frequently terminated in fingered gloves of mail. A new feature appearing at this time was the ailette.

ARMOUR IN THE AGE OF CHIVALRY

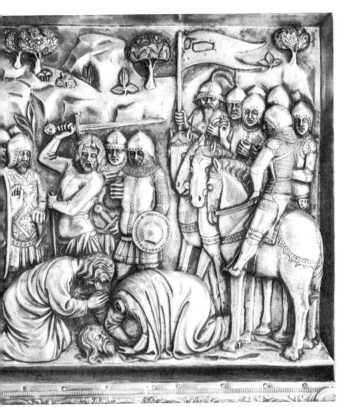

19 and 20 Parts of the silver altar-piece in Pistoia Cathedral completed by Francesco di Niccolò and Leonardo di Ser Giovanni of Florence in 1376, showing deep open-faced helmets and (*above right*) the back straps of a breastplate (*above*)

PROBABLY DUE TO the increasing effectiveness of the English bowman in western Europe and the rise of the professional soldier, the fourteenth century saw a rapid increase in the amount of plate armour worn. The inventory of the goods of Raoul de Nesle, Constable of France, killed at Courtrai in 1302, while mentioning many hauberks and gambesons, includes padded cuisses, arms of leather and iron, gauntlets—one pair covered with red leather—body armours described as *paires de plates*, *plates* and *corsés*, bascinets with their mail tippets (called *camails*), kettle-hats described as *capiaus*, gorgets of mail and of plate, leg harness with greaves and close greaves (that is greaves with back plates), and an *espaulière* of whalebone for the tourney. This represents only that part of the armoury that did not fall into the hands of the victors.

A comparable artistic source is Queen Mary's Psalter (English, early fourteenth century [figure 27]). This shows knights in knee-length surcoats with mail-clad arms and legs, and mail hoods. Most figures have plate poleyns on their knees, and one also wears greaves without backs worn over the mail. Many have their hands protected by old-fashioned mail bag-mittens, while others have bag-mittens apparently not made of mail and with large cuffs, possibly stiffened with strips of whalebone or iron. The contemporary Tickhill Psalter has similar mittens marked all over with rectangles, possibly representing scales or perhaps small plates covered with cloth or leather. In several cases

21 A page from the Maciejowski Bible, French, c. 1250; the waistcoat on the seated figure is possibly some form of body armour

22 The monumental brass of Sir John d'Abernoun in Stoke d'Abernon Church, 1327, showing the beginnings of plate armour on the limbs

23 (*right*) A page from the Manesse Codex, showing arms and equipment for the joust, German, early fourteenth-century

some form of solid shoulder defence is indicated in Queen Mary's Psalter. Small hemispherical bascinets are frequently shown as well as helms, which usually slope back above the sights. Both types are sometimes fitted with movable visors pivoting at the sides. In some cases a helmet similar in shape to the helm is worn, but with an open face: this type is common in Italy throughout the century [figures 19 and 20]. Although kettle-hats or *chapels de fer* are all shown in this

24 The effigy of Don Alveró de Cabrera, erected before 1314 in the monastery of Santa Maria de Bellpuig de las Avellanas at Belaguer, Spain; he wears a reinforced surcoat

25 *Pair of plates*, excavated from the mass graves of the battle of Wisby, in Gotland, fought in 1361

manuscript as made of one piece, the older construction is still illustrated in the Tickhill Psalter.

English monumental brasses of the 'twenties show gutter-shaped plates worn on the arms and lower legs, which were strapped over the mail or held by narrow plate bands hinged to them and encircling the limb [figures 22 and 26]. Occasionally they were riveted to the mail, and a wall painting in South Newington Church, Oxfordshire, shows them laced to it. The feet are usually shown protected by a number of small overlapping plates again over the mail, while small cup-shaped plates, called *couters*, protect the elbows, and circular plates, called *besagews*, are tied or riveted to them and to the shoulders. Continental illustrations frequently show the sleeve of the hauberk worn outside the lower cannon of the arm but beneath the couter and upper cannon defence. The fore-arm is then usually protected only by the aketon, but is sometimes entirely enclosed in plate. This fashion was still popular at the beginning of the second half of the century. Mitten gauntlets and mail coifs still occur. In general, however, finger gauntlets, often apparently of leather or cloth reinforced with plates or whalebone, were fashionable either with wide cuffs like the nineteenth-century cavalry gauntlet, or with gutter-shaped plates strapped over the back of the wrist.

Bascinets were now much more common, either with high pointed skulls or with the more old-fashioned hemispherical skulls, occasionally with a raised ridge running fore and aft over the skull. At first they were apparently worn over the coif, but by the 'twenties brasses show them attached to a mail tippet, called in English the aventail. The most usual method was for the helmet to have staples along its lower edge which passed through holes in the leather attached to the top edge of the mail and a string or wire threaded through the staples above the leather then held mail and helmet together.

Brasses and effigies of this period illustrate a surcoat shorter in front than at the back exposing the lower edge of a garment studded with small florets or circles. Later illus-

26 A page from the Treatise of Walter de Milemete, English, 1326–7; falchions were very commonly used in the early fourteenth century

trations and a number of excavated examples from various European sites indicate that this is a *pair of plates* consisting of numerous small plates riveted to a fabric cover, thus forming a flexible body armour. Beneath this the hauberk is often visible, and beneath that the skirts of the aketon. The reinforced surcoat is still occasionally found, as on the effigy of Don Alvaró de Cabrera, Viscount of Ager, erected before 1314 [figure 24]. The head of this figure is only protected by a coif of mail, the face-opening of which is bound with a thong, perhaps to stiffen the edge of the mail or to attach a lining. Some German effigies show fabric-lined coifs while others show that the mail is not lined. The de Cabrera effigy shows the first example of closed greaves, and a gorget with a tippet apparently made on the same principle as the surcoat, while the upper cannons of the arms and the feet are also shown as if constructed in this way. Representations of similar collars, as in the Walter de Milemete manuscript of 1326–7, indicate that they were worn with kettle-hats [figure 26]. This manuscript also appears to show aventails made of many horizontal lames which also appear to be depicted in the Lorenzetti *Allegory of Good Government* at Siena (1338–1339). The latter shows a form of visor which pivots at the sides and only covers the face below the eyes.

The Milemete manuscript not only includes the earliest known illustration of a cannon, but also shows siege engines, the bombardment of a town with hives of bees and an aerial bombardment with fire-bombs from a dragon-shaped kite.

A few effigies of the 'forties show body armour of small plates apparently worn without a cover, visible beneath the coat armour, as the surcoat was called. These plates are presumably attached to a fabric or leather lining, and armour of this type is referred to in contemporary documents. *The Romance of Alexander* in the Bodleian Library (1338–44) shows the back views of two figures wearing *plates* without coat armour. The construction of the *plates* differs very little from the reinforced surcoat of the St Maurice figure at Magdeburg, the side wings passing under the arm and buckling or tying together at the centre back. A figure on the Levitic pew in Verden Cathedral (c. 1360–70) shows that the area above the wings at the back was also protected by lames. The majority of the *pairs of plates* excavated from graves on the site of the battle of Wisby, 1361, are of this construction [figure 25].

None of the Wisby armours has a solid breastplate, but a group of German effigies of the middle of the century show

27 A battle scene from Queen Mary's Psalter, English, c. 1300

that the top part of the *plates* covering the upper breast was now made in one piece, with small laminations over the shoulder, and a saucer- or shell-shaped plate protecting the point of the shoulder. A number of chains attached to the upper breast prevent the sword, dagger and helm from being lost in action [figure 30]. By 1360 this plate covered the whole chest [figure 34] and by the following decade the breastplate was complete. The skirt is usually represented with horizontal rows of studs, presumably representing narrow horizontal lames riveted to the cover, as on a surviving breastplate and fauld at Munich.

Although literary evidence of independent breastplates is fairly common from *c.* 1340, it is not until the 'seventies that effigies occur wearing a large separate plate over the *pair of plates* [figure 31]. Both in Germany and Italy this separate plate is occasionally worn independently with a short laminated apron covering the stomach. Back views are rare, but the silver altarpiece in Pistoia Cathedral (before 1376) and the St George at Basle (*c.* 1390) show straps crossing the back of the body [figure 19]. The Munich breast and fauld, however, have lace holes down both sides and shoulder attachments, suggesting a plate back defence. The frescoes

28 (*opposite*) The helm which was hung over the tomb of Sir Richard Pembridge (*d.* 1375), formerly in Hereford Cathedral, and now in the Royal Scottish Museum, Edinburgh

29 (below, right) The effigy of Walter von Hohenklingen from Feldbach, Switzerland

30 (below) The effigy of Otto von Orlamünde (d. 1340) in the Convent Church at Himmelkron, Bavaria; the body armour is a *pair of plates*, the chains on the breast are to attach the helm and weapons

by Altichiero in St George's chapel, Padua, show a side view of a cuirass similar in construction to the Munich one but with a back defence apparently formed entirely of small cloth-covered plates. A number of the cuirasses in these frescoes open down the centre front. The effigy of Walter von Hohenklingen, killed at Sempach in 1386, shows a breastplate worn over a quilted tunic with long baggy sleeves

31 The effigy of Dieter von Hohenberg (d. 1381) from Burg Homberg, Bavaria, Germany

[figure 29]. Many representations of this period, particularly of German knights, show only quilted body defences with no visible breastplate [figure 33]. A gambeson or quilted coat armour of Charles VI of France when Dauphin is in Chartres Museum.

One of the earliest surviving pieces at Schloss Churburg is a breastplate designed to be worn without a skirt, but clearly descended from a *pair of plates*. It consists of nine vertical plates on a leather lining, the centre three covering the breast, the remainder extending under the arms and held by straps crossing the spine. It is fitted with a folding lance-rest and not only is the top edge turned over to prevent a weapon sliding off the edge of the plate into the throat, but a V-shaped bar is riveted on below this as an added precaution [figure 45]. A similar breastplate occurs on the effigy of Konrad von Bickenbach, who died in 1393 [figure 32].

Leg-harness developed gradually throughout the century. In Germany particularly there seems to have been less uniformity than elsewhere, mail still playing a prominent part. Sometimes, instead of greaves, splints were strapped over the mail on each side of the calf and down the shin. In the remainder of Europe, quilted cuisses were replaced from the '50s by others made apparently on the principle of the *pair of plates*, and after c. 1370 plate cuisses became common. The poleyn developed small circular side wings to protect the muscles inside the joint. At first they were strapped over the cuisse as before, later they were attached to it. By the end of the century, the normal form of defence for the upper leg consisted of a large plate protecting the front of the thigh hinged to a vertical side plate protecting the outside of the leg. To the bottom of the main lame was riveted the poleyn or its articulating lame: these were free to pivot. The poleyn usually had a kidney- or heart-shaped wing. Another lame below the poleyn strapped over the top of the greave, and was often attached to it by means of a slot and a turning pin. Horizontally laminated cuisses are occasionally shown later in the century and a horizontal stop-rib was often fixed near the top to protect the groin from a weapon sliding up the cuisse. Sabatons usually consisted of horizontal lames, but scale-covered shoes are sometimes represented. In Chartres Museum there survives the leg of an armour of Charles VI of France as a boy which retains part of the silver-gilt decoration on the edge of the sabaton.

By the middle of the century, an almost standard arm

23

32 (*above*) The effigy of Konrad von Bickenbach (*d.* 1393) from Grüblingen bei Obernburg, Germany

33 (*left*) St. George, from a French, late fourteenth-century manuscript in the British Museum; his body-armour is a quilted gambeson

34 The tomb of the Chevalier Mahiu de Montmorency at Tavergny, France, 1360 (after F. de Guilhermy), the *pair of plates* has a solid breast

complex had been adopted in Western Europe. The couter, usually with a circular wing, was articulated to the upper and lower cannon by means of narrow, articulating lames [figures 36 and 45]. The point of the shoulder was defended by a series of small horizontal lames, and a besagew or rondel was hung in front. The ailettes were still occasionally worn until the middle of the fourteenth century. Towards the end of the century, the shoulder defence sometimes consisted of a large plate defending the point of the shoulder, articulated to the upper arm by one or more narrow lames. The besagew was now rarer. In Germany the arm defences were frequently tied to the under-garment by means of arming laces, and this remained the most normal construction throughout the following century. Italy was slow to adopt plate arm defences and even in the second half of the century the shoulder was frequently only protected by the short mail sleeve of the hauberk [figure 35]. By this time a satisfactory form of gauntlet had been developed in which the cuff and back of the hand were covered by a simple wasp-waisted plate which completely encircled the wrist, and each finger was covered by a row of small overlapping scales.

The small hemispherical bascinet remained popular in Italy and France throughout the century, but a tall conical type was also worn there, and in Northern Europe this was by far the most popular type. Examples of intermediate height are common and, particularly in Germany towards the end of the century, ogival skulls are often found. Painting and sculpture give a somewhat misleading idea of the shape of these helmets since surviving specimens are frequently much deeper than the level of the vervelles, the lower part being invisible beneath the mail. In Italy particularly, bascinets of all sorts were often worn without aventails. Those of the foot soldiers frequently offered little or no protection to the back of the neck, but those of the better armed often had a deep skirt covering the neck and partly encircling the face. The visor is rarely found on this type but one example occurs at Paris. The commonest form of visor remained that pivoted at the side, but in Germany it was frequently hung from the centre of the brow of the helmet. A Bohemian altarpiece of *c.* 1380 shows a grille face-guard attached in this way. From the middle of the century the visor began to have an angular profile, presumably to provide an improved glancing surface away from the face. Both in Italy and Germany the visor was often replaced by

25

35 The effigy of Jacopo dei Cavalli (*d*. 1384) in SS Giovanni e Paolo, Venice; note the absence of plate shoulder defences and the cloth cover to the aventail

a metal nasal attached to the aventail which in action hooked to the brow of the helmet. Towards the end of the century the peak of the skull moved backwards until the back of the helmet was almost perpendicular. The visor pivots were made so that the visor was easily removed, and the visor itself developed a large conical projection over the nose [figure 45]. Until the end of the century, the helm was still occasionally worn over the bascinet and in a headpiece such as that of Sir Richard Pembridge (*d*. 1375) pierced with broad sights and numerous breaths, visibility is very little restricted [figure 28]. The kettle-hat was still popular and was sometimes worn in addition to the bascinet as in the Bodleian *Romance of Alexander*.

The sports used in order to accustom young soldiers to battle must be nearly as old as war itself. Throughout the Middle Ages we have numerous accounts of mimic combats between groups of cavalry, called tournaments, between individual horsemen, called *justes* or jousts, or between dismounted men within the barriers, the fenced-in area where the fight took place. In the eleventh and twelfth centuries, as far as we know, the weapons employed were the weapons used in war and such was the loss of life that successive

36 The gilt bronze effigy of Edward the Black Prince (*d*. 1376) in Canterbury Cathedral

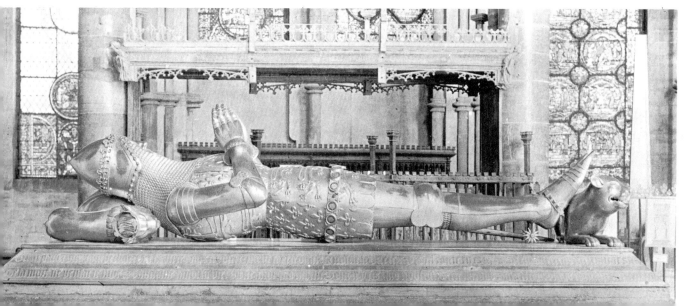

Popes banned the tournament and many of the wiser kings tried to suppress it in their own lands. Between 1272 and 1348 forty-one prohibitions were issued in England alone.

By the thirteenth century blunt lances were in use in some of the mounted duels, but in others sharp lances were still used. For the Windsor Tournament of 1278, which appears to have been a *mêlée* fought with whalebone swords, the accounts for the purchase of armour survive. It was all of leather and consisted of chanfrons, that is head coverings for the horses, ailettes, quiretis (body armour), shields, helms, the last either silvered or gilt according to rank, and finally crests.

In the fourteenth century armour designed specially for the joust occurs not only in the many surviving inventories and wills but is also visible in contemporary illustrations. The Manesse Codex of the early years of the century shows the lance for the joust of peace with triple-pointed head, called a coronell, and the circular vamplate before the hand. The helm is shown with a steel wrapper round the neck and lower face to guard the throat [figure 23]. The saddles have rolls of cloth in front to defend the thighs, which also occur in the Milemete manuscript. The shield is already shown tied to the shoulder by means of laces.

As early as 1322 the Inventory of the effects of Roger de Mortimer distinguishes between helms for war, those for the joust and those for the tournament, but it is not until the Bodleian *Romance of Alexander* that the difference between war and joust helms is distinguishable to us. The war helms in this manuscript continue to have a bar between the eyes joining the brow to the face-plate, while the majority of joust helms have no bar and the lower edge of the sight is placed in advance of the upper edge, foreshadowing the frog-mouthed helms of the following century. They were worn as before with a wrapper. This manuscript shows saddles for the joust with leg defences consisting of large, rectangular wings to the saddle-bow which are not found on the war saddles. Towards the end of this century, the Oranse Manuscript at Vienna shows the riders lifted high off their horses' backs in special saddles with deep guards for the legs and with arms reaching round the thighs from the back of the seat.

In 1341 a complete armour for the joust was delivered to Edward III of England by his armourer, Gerard de Tourney. It consisted of a helm with a wrapper (called a *barber*), a *pair of plates*, a breastplate, a pair of arms, a maindefer,

37 Miniature from the *Romance of Alexander*, Flemish, dated 1338–44, showing the commencement of a battle

four vamplates and six coronells. The Register of Edward the Black Prince makes it clear that *plates* and a breastplate were the normal wear for jousting at this time. No fourteenth-century illustration of a 'maindefer' has so far been recorded but early fifteenth-century illuminations such as the British Museum's *Buke of John Mandeuill* (c. 1410–20) already show a heavy, left-hand gauntlet with an elbow-length cuff in use. Many contemporary illustrations show jousters without leg armour but as no special type was required, when it was used it was probably taken from a field armour in the owner's armoury. By the end of the century, the joust helm was securely buckled to breast and back. For courses with sharp lances and for combat on foot in the barriers the ordinary field armour was worn.

IN THE FIFTEENTH CENTURY two major styles emerge,

38 and 39 Armour and equipment for the joust, also from the *Romance of Alexander*

WAR AND TOURNAMENTS
IN THE EARLY RENAISSANCE

40 Horse armour made by Pier Innocenzo da Faerno, Milan, c. 1450

that of Germany, spiky and broken in outline and surface in keeping with Northern Gothic taste, and that of Italy, rounded and smooth, employing simple lines and large surfaces in the Renaissance taste. Both areas, especially in the latter part of the century, enjoyed a wide export trade and produced armours to suit the fashions of other lands. Elsewhere, styles seem to derive from either German or Italian fashions, modified according to the needs and tastes of each area.

The great Italian centre was Milan, where many hundreds of armourers worked. The work of a few of them has been identified by means of their marks struck on the metal. The most famous of all, the Missaglia family, built up a great commercial business employing many specialist craftsmen and with agents abroad. Many Milanese armourers emigrated and many have been traced working for the French court at Tours, in England and in Flanders.

At the German centres of Augsburg, Landshut, Nurem-

41 Effigy of Jörg Truchsess von Waldburg (d. 1467) in the Church of Waldsee, Württemberg; a German armour showing slight Italian influence in the breastplate and tassets

berg and, later, Innsbruck, the armourers worked in small workshops employing a few craftsmen and apprentices.

As with so many mediaeval 'mysteries', no treatise on the making of armour has survived. However, a little can be discovered from the few surviving illustrations of armourers at work, and from the experience of modern restorers. The iron arrived at the workshop in the form of billets, and,

The defences of the arms were either of the Italian form or consisted of separate upper and lower cannons, joined by straps, and a large shell-shaped couter attached by harness points to the arming doublet. The shoulder was usually defended by a number of small lames, with a larger one over the point of the shoulder to which was attached a movable besagew. By the 'thirties the larger plate was often extended downwards to cover the armhole. This gradually became the standard pauldron in the German lands and in the sixteenth century was almost universal.

Leg harness remained much the same as before, but there was a tendency for the poleyn wings to be decorated with radiating flutes which are also found on the couter wings.

Italian influence became increasingly strong as the century progressed. Many German sculptures and paintings show armours with Italian features, such as shield-shaped tassets, and reinforces to the pauldrons. In the second half of the century the rounded form of cuirass became widespread, often with two or more placates. These southern features were married to a purely northern decorative scheme. Frequently the surface of all the plates was fluted, and wherever the flutes reached the edge of a plate the metal was drawn out into a point. As the end of the century approached, the flutes swirled over the surface in the last although most of the great centres of armour-manufacture were situated in iron-bearing districts, a brisk export trade existed from Germany, Lombardy and Spain to centres less fortunate.

Contemporary illustrations, such as the early sixteenth-century *Weisskunig* illustrated by Hans Burgkmair and the *Hausbuch des Mendelschen Zwölfbruderhauses*, show armourers working the cold metal held in their bare hands. Conrad Seusenhofer's bench in the *Weisskunig* is littered with the stakes or small anvils over which the metal was worked by means of a variety of different hammers. Although at first all the hammer-work was done by hand, later the preliminary work was probably carried out by a water-driven trip-hammer, such as is shown in Jan Breughel the Elder's

Forge of Venus in the Palazzo Doria, Rome. Great care was taken to make the metal thickest over the most vulnerable spot and the left side of an armour of good quality was often made heavier than the right. The forge in the background of two of these pictures is ready for the frequent annealing required during the working of the metal from the billet to the finished plate. Heat was also required when the raised ribs at the edge of the plates were formed by bending the plate round a wire. A huge pair of shears fixed in a block of wood served for trimming the edge of the finished plate. The armour was then rough from the hammer, black and covered with the dimple marks of the blows. It was then sent to be glazed in the water- or horse-driven harness mill, where the surface was polished by swiftly rotating wheels. Genuine armour almost invariably shows the dimple marks of the hammer on the interior. Particularly in the fifteenth century, many armours were finished with a blued oxidised surface. The plates were attached to each other by means of rivets loosely closed so that the plates were free to move. The lames fitted tightly enough to prevent gaps appearing when fully flexed but, to make sure, each plate was usually riveted to a leather strap running along the axis of the defence on the inside. Hinges of brass were riveted on the outside of the plates where necessary, but, latterly, internal steel hinges were used as being less likely to be damaged. Where it was necessary to open a defence to put the armour on, the plate was usually locked shut by means of spring pins which were sometimes further secured by a sneck. Although the larger shops could afford to employ a locksmith to make their hinges and fastenings, examination of surviving armours suggests that the trade was supplied by a few large specialist merchants.

The completed armour was fitted with a padded lining in such parts as the helmet, the breast, tassets and cuisses. In the late sixteenth and in the seventeenth centuries, the edges of the lining usually appear beyond the edges of the plates as a series of scallops of coloured cloth, known as pickadils [figure 67]. These helped to prevent the plates scratching each other.

From about the middle of the fourteenth century we find references in documents to armour of proof, that is armour certified as being proof against contemporary weapons. It was at first tested by means of cross-bows and later by fire-arms. The dent caused by the testing bullet is frequently to be seen on seventeenth-century breastplates. Armourers

42 Memorial brass to Thomas Lord Camoys KG and his wife, dated 1419, Trotton Church, Sussex

43 A unique form of the armet, *c.* 1430; it bears the mark attributed to Tomasso dei Negroni da Ello detto Missaglia of Milan (the visor is missing)

44 Miniature from the Poems of Christine de Pisan, French, *c.* 1415; the bascinet is fitted with a single gorget plate

signed their work by means of a stamp struck on the surface of the metal. The marks of Milan normally consist of initials beneath crosses or crowns, although the Negroli family used a stamp representing crossed keys. German marks are usually symbolic or heraldic; thus the mark of Matthes Deutsch was a plane leaf and that of Lorenz Helmschmied a helm with a cross as a crest. The German towns also placed a view mark on the armour indicating that the piece had passed the viewers appointed by the municipality.

Although armours could be bought ready-made in the shops of retailers, and many merchants seemed to have added a few stands of armour to their mixed cargoes when trading overseas, the well-to-do normally ordered their suits from a specialist armourer who made them to their measurements. Great care was taken to ensure an accurate fit, and we know that in some cases the customer's garments were sent to the armourer as a pattern. Small plates showing alternative designs to be used in decorating his armours were sent from Germany to Philip II in Spain so that he might make his final choice. A number of them have survived in the Real Armería, Madrid. Most great nobles attached a permanent armourer to their household to attend them in the field and at the tournament, who would clean and maintain their armours and make minor alterations and adjustments, such as those required by increasing corpulence. Only in the greatest courts would this man actually make armours.

The hauberk was still worn under the armour until the end of the fifteenth century, particularly in Italy, where its sleeves and skirt often appear respectively beneath the edges of the pauldrons and fauld. It was, however, increasingly common for the mail shirt to be replaced by a mail gorget and skirt, and by gussets of mail attached to the arming doublet inside the elbows and at the armholes to close the gaps in the plates. Except under the jousting helm, and occasionally under the salet, the independent arming-cap was replaced by a lining padded with grass or wool and fixed to the inside of the helmet.

Soon after the beginning of the fifteenth century, the armour of plate was completed by the use of a backplate and by the universal adoption of a gorget attached to the bascinet, in place of the aventail. Early backplates were often made of two plates buckled together at the centre, but later a one-piece back was adopted. The tight fitting coat armour went out of fashion, but a wide variety of harness coats were worn throughout the century.

45 The armour of a Vogt of Matsch, in Schloss Churburg ,Tyrol; Milanese, *c.* 1390

46 Effigy of Kunz von Haberkorn (*d.* 1421) from the Johanniterordenskirche at Würzburg, Bavaria; note the rather unusual skirt of scales

47 Model of the tomb of Duke Ludwig of Bayern-Ingolstadt by Hans Multscher, 1435, showing an armour in the German fashion

Now that the armour of plate was completed, the armourers of northern Italy worked throughout the century to perfect it. From about 1420 onwards the breast and back were made in two parts divided horizontally, the lower part overlapping the upper part and strapped to it. This is first seen on the effigy of Giovanni Cose (d. 1418) in the Louvre, and in an armour at Schloss Churburg in the South Tyrol. Surviving cuirasses are, or have been, hinged down the left side and buckled down the right. Throughout the century the lower part of the breastplate, the placate, became more pointed at the centre and increased in size until it eventually covered the whole breast. It was usually buckled to the breastplate at the centre top, but one variety, with a fish-tail outline to the top of the placate, was held by two straps emerging from the arm holes. The lower part of the backplate also became more pointed and increased slightly in size, while from the middle of the century the upper part was usually laminated horizontally, but occasionally vertically. From about 1430 additional plates, called tassets, were hung from the bottom of the fauld in front of the thighs, and a little later similar, but smaller, additional plates were added at the sides and rear [figures 57 and 59].

Although until about 1420 plate shoulder defences were rare in Italy, the Cose effigy shows large, horizontally laminated pauldrons. The right one was invariably smaller at the front to allow the lance to be couched beneath this arm. A large circular reinforce was placed in front of the more vulnerable left shoulder, but soon reinforces shaped to fit the front of the pauldrons were fitted by means of staples and split pins on both shoulders [figures 58 and 59]. The large back wings were at first nearly rectangular but by the 'seventies they were pointed and overlapped at the back, as on the San Severino armour at Vienna (before 1487).

Basically, there was little change in the armour of the limbs except that the couter and poleyn wings increased in size and curved round to protect the joint. From about 1440 the left couter was covered by a large reinforcing plate called 'the guard of the vambrace'. The gauntlet cuffs became very long and pointed and the fingers were protected by a single, broad lame.

During the second decade of the century an entirely new headpiece, the armet, appeared in Italy and remained popular well into the following century [figure 43]. The earliest complete example to survive, dating from about 1440, consists of a hemispherical skull hinged to which are two side

48 Breastplate of the German fashion and lower cannons of the arms, probably made at Innsbruck, c. 1450–60

49 Portions of an armour, probably of Gaudenz Vogt von Matsch at Schloss Churburg, made by Christian Treytz, c. 1490

plates locking together at the chin. The back joint of these two plates is protected by a narrow tail extending downwards from the skull. A small, pointed, removable visor falls over the side plates, the sight being formed by the gap between the top of the visor and the bottom edge of the skull. The area of the brow is reinforced by an additional plate. A mail aventail was attached to the lower edge of the helmet, and the front was protected by a wrapper which strapped round the neck. The straps were supported by a pin projecting from the tail of the skull and were defended by a rondel on the end of the pin.

A second, very popular form of helmet was the deep open-faced salet derived from the bascinet. Until the last quarter of the century the face opening was often made very narrow, leaving only a T-shaped opening. In the early sixteenth century this type of helmet was frequently fitted with a visor of bellows form [figure 62].

In Germany, on the whole, there was slightly less interest in complete armours of plate. Early in the century the commonest arming was still a breastplate, often of rather baggy profile, worn occasionally with a skirt of plate but often only with a mail fauld. By the 'thirties a very deep, bell-shaped skirt of plate became popular, worn with a breastplate in which the bagging had become angular and box-like. The head-piece was usually a kettle-hat, sometimes with a sight pierced through the deep brim, or a bascinet with gorget plates and a visor with rounded snout. The second was the most common form of helmet in the remainder of north-western Europe. After c. 1430 a closely fitting collar of plates was often worn with the kettle-hat, becoming more popular until c. 1500 when it was universally adopted. flowering of High Gothic. The edges of the plates were pierced with designs based on the fleur-de-lys or were decorated with bands of chiselled gilt brass. Laminations multiplied at all joints to form an armour of great flexibility [figures 41 and 52].

The German salet developed from the kettle-hat by the drawing out of the back edge of the brim to a long point. The front was often made as a separate visor. Italian export armours for the German market had more rounded forms of the salet, which were also the type most popular in north-western Europe. As with the kettle-hat, the chin was defended by a plate bevor often attached to the breastplate.

Many German armours of the third quarter of the century have very short skirts worn with mail breeches and leg-armour with numerous laminations stretching up onto the hips. The little armour of Philip the Fair by Hans Prunner of Innsbruck at Vienna shows the short laminated tassets coming into use in the late 'eighties.

Paintings of armour in north-eastern Italy and surviving armours made at Innsbruck, show the interaction of the two fashions across the Brenner Pass towards the end of the century [figures 49 and 62]. France seems to have followed Italian fashions, while in Flanders and the Iberian

50 Armour for the German course with sharp lances, made *c.* 1490 for the Emperor Maximilian I by Christian Treytz of Mühlau, near Innsbruck

51 The Milanese armour of Count Galeazzo da Arco, at Schloss Churburg, by Tomasso dei Negroni detto Missaglia, *c.* 1445

52 Portions of an armour of the Emperor Maximilian I, when Archduke, made by Lorenz Helmschmied of Augsburg in 1480

53 Armour for the German joust of the Archduke Sigismund of Tyrol, made by Kaspar Rieder of Mühlau, near Innsbruck, c. 1485–90

Peninsula there was some blending of the two major styles. In Spain and Portugal, and to a lesser extent in Flanders, the cuirass and pauldrons were very frequently made of brigandine, and kettle-hats were very popular.

In the last quarter of the century the initiative in technical developments was gained by the Imperial Armourer, Lorenz Helmschmied (1445–1516), under the patronage of Maximilian I. The latter's interest in every form of tournament is shown by such publications as *Freydal*, *Theuer-*

dank, and *The Triumph of Maximilian*. The inventiveness of Helmschmied is shown in the Thun Sketchbook, probably some kind of pictorial record of his work, and by his surviving armours [figure 52]. From these Dr Ortwin Gamber has been able to reconstruct the great garniture of the Emperor Maximilian I, probably purchased in 1492. This included a field armour and a saddle, a foot-combat armour with a salet and an armet, an armour in the Italian fashion, an armour for the *Kampfrennen* (a rare course with sharp lances), an armour for the course with sharp lances and swords in the west-European fashion, and an armour for the Italian course with sharp lances with an exchange helmet for the Italian joust. Here Helmschmied has brought together the ideas and inventions of many nations and combined them as a set of matching armours with pieces of exchange, foreshadowing the great garnitures of the following century. These elegant, light, flexible harnesses demonstrate his remarkable skill. Defence is not merely by weight of metal but by its extreme tensile strength and by the skilful arrangement of the planes of the surface to lead a weapon away from vital points.

So much material for a history of the tournament in the fifteenth century exists in the form of challenges, memoirs, chronicles and even detailed descriptions of the armour to be used, as well as illustrations, that it is impossible to do more than generalise here. The principal types of combat popular at the beginning of the century were mounted duels with blunt lances in the special armour with shield and frog-mouthed helm, or with sharp lances in field armour, the *mêlée*, in which two groups of cavalry fought, and a variety of foot-combats usually in the form of a duel but occasionally as a *mêlée*.

In the 1420s a barrier known as the tilt was introduced between the contestants in the mounted duel to prevent the horses colliding. The tilters rode along opposite sides of the barrier keeping their shield sides towards each other, their lances crossing their horses' necks and the tilt. This innovation never became universal and many courses, particularly those using sharp lances, were run 'at random', that is in the open field. Towards the end of the century a barrier was also introduced for some foot-combats: Henry VIII of England was apparently particularly keen on this type of contest and practised it regularly.

The joust with blunt lances continued without very much change throughout the century. The object was usually to

54 A shield bearing the arms of the town of Deggendorf, *c.* 1440–50

55 Foot-combat armour of Claude de Vaudrey, Chamberlain of Burgundy, by Giovanni Marco Meraviglia and Damiano dei Negroni detto Missaglia; Milanese, c 1500

break lances, but in some forms the aim was to unhorse one's opponent. In Germany, as lances became heavier, a long arm with a hook at the end, known as a queue, was bolted to the right side of the breast and projected behind in order to steady the butt of the lance. This form of duel was usually run in a normal joust saddle but in Germany the very high encircling saddle of the Oranse Manuscript continued to be used occasionally, perhaps as a conscious piece of antiquarianism. In another form the front of the horse was protected by a large, crescent-shaped bolster hung from the saddle bow. Although in Germany the cuirass was invariably of steel [figure 53], in England, Spain and France, particularly, a cuirass of brigandine was still occasionally used as in the fourteenth century. The *mêlée* with blunt lances was also fought in this type of armour.

This kind of joust was continued in the sixteenth century, but latterly a rather different form of armour was used. The helmet was a close-helmet but was bolted to the cuirass to keep it rigid, the queue was given up, and the leather- or horn-covered targe was replaced by a steel one bolted to the breast over the left shoulder [figure 63]. Alternatively, in place of the targe, a reinforce covering and enclosing the front of the left shoulder was bolted to the breastplate. In both cases a large reinforce was worn over the left elbow and a heavy bridle-gauntlet, the maindefer, was used.

The courses with sharp lances were usually run in a field armour with either a salet or, more usually, an armet. By the middle of the century special reinforces had already been devised for the left side of the armour. In the combat between Lord Scales and the Bastard of Burgundy in 1467, we read that as soon as the lance course was over the former discarded the wrapper of his helmet and the reinforces of his left shoulder and elbow. This discarding of the guards is actually illustrated in the Lucas Cranach *Tournament of the Sampson Tapestry* of 1509 [endpapers]. Such reinforced armour was also used for the *mêlée* with sharp lances and swords, the reinforces being cast aside for the later part. The normal tilt armour of western Europe in the sixteenth century derived from this and usually consisted of a field armour with the addition of a large left elbow-reinforce, a maindefer and a large reinforce to the left pauldron, called a grandguard, which sometimes covered the front of the helmet and was attached to the breastplate.

In Germany, a second form of combat with sharp lances was also practised with the aim of unhorsing one's op-

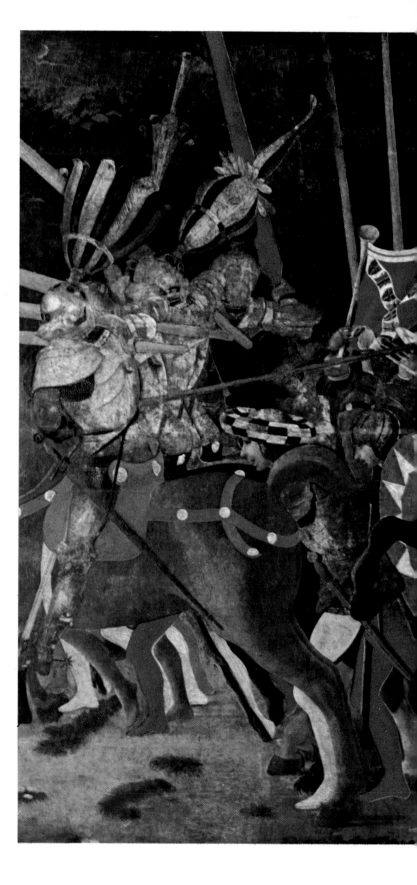

56 (*above*) Effigy of Don García Osorio (*d.* after 1502) from San Pedro, Orcaña, near Aranjuez, Spain, probably erected before his death

57 (*right*) Part of the *Rout of San Romano* by Paolo Uccello, *c.* 1450, Louvre, Paris

58 St Florian wearing an Italian armour, from an altar-piece of the Madonna and Saints by Bernardino and Francesco Zaganelli, 1499

ponent or tearing off his shield. The armour used was based on the lightest of field armours used by the German light cavalry, and consisted of a salet and bevor, a breastplate and a very large, leather shield [figure 50]. Arm-defences were usually dispensed with, the shield and a large vamplate making them unneccessary. The saddle normally had no back and the thighs were protected by two large circular or shield-shaped plates hung loosely over the saddle bow. Leg armour was not usually worn. The queue for the lance was also used in this armour. Towards the end of the century innumerable varieties of this course were developed at the Imperial Court including those with shields which exploded on impact, apparently in imitation of the bursting of an old-fashioned, wooden shield. Latterly, the lances employed for these courses had fairly obtuse points and were not nearly as lethal as those used for war.

The *mêlée* with swords and clubs, or more rarely with battle-axes, was fought in a form of bascinet fixed to the cuirass and with a face grille of vertical bars. The contestants sat in high, encircling saddles similar to those of the Oranse Manuscript. The armour and organisation of such a tournament is described and illustrated in the *Traictié de la forme et devis d'ung Tournoy* by King René of Anjou (*c*. 1460). The club tournament did not survive the fifteenth century, and, as far as is known at present, the last one took place at Worms in 1487, but illustrations and instructions found their way into heralds' manuals for another hundred years. In all forms of *mêlée* the contestants were attended by squires and foot varlets to assist them if they were dismounted, and to drag them out of the press.

The foot-combats, such as those described by Olivier de la Marche in his *Memoires*, were, until nearly the end of the century, fought in normal field armours without the lance rest. The choice of combinations of armour appears normally to have been left to the contestants. The usual weapons were casting spear, polaxe or *bec-de-corbin*, sword and dagger. A shield was carried but was normally hurled at one's opponent before taking to the axe. The Emperor Maximilian's tournament book *Freydal*, however, shows glaives, maces, falchions, boar spear and buckler, war-hammers, throwing hammers and even flails in use. The number of blows was often limited and they were delivered by each contestant in turn. Occasionally the challenge states that the fight is to continue until one or other was borne to the earth. English challenges sometimes include archery contests, wrestling and casting the bar. Two special forms of foot-combat armour appeared towards the end of the century and remained in vogue during the first half of the sixteenth century. One had a completely enclosing breech of plate and was probably intended for the combat with axes, the other had a tonlet, a great, wide, bell-shaped skirt of horizontal steel lames, and was apparently used for the combat with two-handed sword or hand-and-a-half sword and buckler [figures 55 and 72].

It is difficult to describe the organization of a typical tournament since each differed enormously in detail. In general, however, a challenge would be issued by an individual or a group of people, the Defenders, to all comers to meet them in certain forms of combat at a set place and time. The challenge was often very elaborate and was based on a complicated fiction such as the *Pas de l'Arbre d'Or* held in 1468 to celebrate the marriage of the Duke of Burgundy with the Princess Margaret, sister of Edward IV of England. The Articles of the Tournament, that is the rules to be followed and the descriptions of the combats chosen and the prizes, was published by proclamation throughout the realm and sometimes in foreign courts.

At the place appointed the lists would be laid out and sanded, a scaffolding with seats for the judge or judges and for the court would be built and decorated with foliage and textile hangings. Pavilions would be erected in which the contestants could arm. At one end of the lists a tall object such as a tree, a unicorn or a lily would be set up, and on this would be hung different coloured shields, each signifying a different combat. On the appointed day those who accepted the challenge, the Comers, touched the shields representing the combats in which they wished to take part. The heralds would then record their names and arms. The Defenders would take it in turns to meet one of the Comers. During the fight trumpeters and drummers played and guns were fired. The judge was assisted in keeping the score by the heralds and pursuivants, and, if he thought that the fight was becoming too dangerous, he could throw down his baton or arrow, the sign of his authority, and order the guards of the Constable or Marshal of the lists to separate the combatants. Olivier de la Marche frequently mentions contestants being forcibly parted.

All the combats of one kind might take place on the same day or during one week, or they might be fought alternately with the other combats of the challenge. In a few cases

tournaments lasted for a whole year, although fighting only took place on one or two days of each month and only the Defenders would be in constant attendance.

Sometimes on the last day of the tournament, some special combat was held in which all those who had already taken part fought again. This usually took the form of a mounted *mêlée* or the defence and assault on foot of an imitation castle. Finally there was a great banquet with many elaborate courses with Interludes acted between them. The prizes were then awarded usually consisting of jewels or weapons either of gold or at least gilt. At the Tournament of the *Chevalier Sauvage à la Dame noire*, held in Edinburgh in 1508, the final banquet at Holyroodhouse lasted three days, from nine in the morning until nine at night, and on the last night 'thair come ane clwdd out of the rwffe of the hall ... and opnit and cleikit up the black lady in presence of thame all that scho was no moir seine ..'. This was achieved by the art of magic of Andro Forman, Bishop of Murray.

Fatalities in tournaments were by no means rare; Henry VIII of England was nearly killed in 1524 as a result of failing to lower his visor, and in 1559 Henry II of France died of a wound received in the tilt-yard.

59 *St George* by Andrea Mantegna in the Accademia, Venice, showing a north Italian armour of *c*. 1460

THE FINEST ACHIEVEMENTS IN ARMOUR-DESIGN

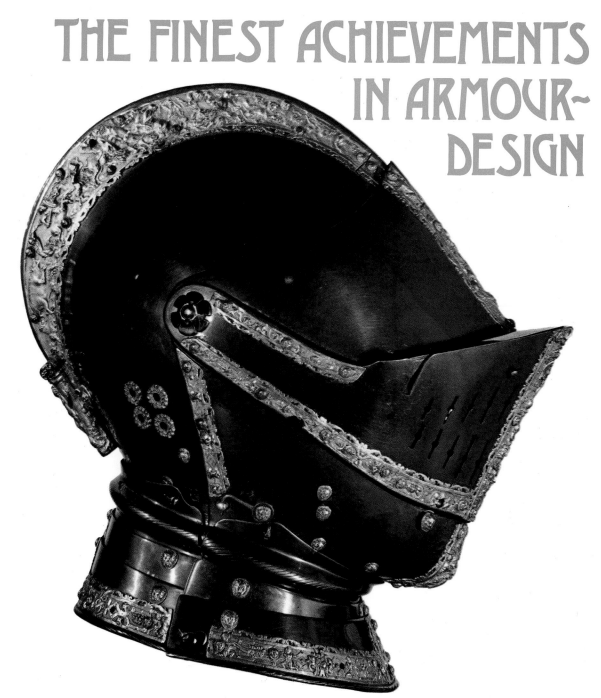

60 The helmet of the 'Blue and Gold' garniture of the future Emperor Maximilian II, south German, probably Augsburg, dated 1557

THE SIXTEENTH CENTURY saw the culmination of the union of round, Italian forms with the technical and structural features of German armour.

At this time, the head piece of the full armour normally consisted of a close-helmet derived from the Italian armet, or from the salet with the addition of a chin plate pivoting on the visor pivots, or from the late fifteenth-century German armet rotating on top of the gorget. The breastplate was

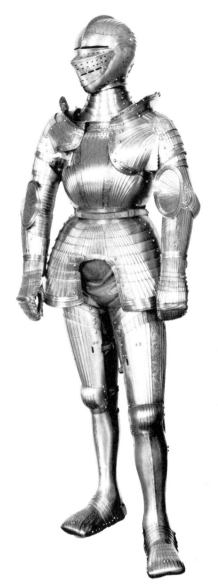

rounded and rather globose, and the skirt swelled out from the waist in a matching curve. The arms were sometimes of the German, sometimes of the Italian construction. The gauntlets were almost always of mitten form with a straight upper edge to the cuff, both stronger than earlier types and more in keeping with the robust forms of contemporary fashion. The sabatons were invariably shaped like the broad-toed, contemporary shoe. The edges of all plates tended to be finished with sunk bands and a light ridge, the latter frequently decorated with roping. The German armourers now more frequently used the Italian type of couter, already adopted by the Helmschmied family at the end of the previous century, while Italian armourers increasingly made the German type already in use in the Venetian area by *c.* 1490. Italian examples are invariably riveted, rather than tied, to the leather joining together the upper and lower cannons. Although the armours of this style made in Italy usually have smooth surfaces, those made in the German lands were decorated all over with numerous flutes, sometimes arranged in groups divided by plain areas [figure 61]. Armours in this fluted style do occur in Italian paintings, particularly in the Venetian area where German influence was particularly strong at this time, and one, probably made for a member of the French court, has survived at Paris. It bears the mark attributed to Giovanni Angelo Missaglia, one of the last of this great family of armourers. On the other hand, Italian paintings and sculpture continue to show a style of armour clearly derived from late fifteenth-century fashions, differing from them only in the shape of the sabatons, the blunter form of the gauntlets and the division of the tassets into three horizontal lames. Again an armour of this type has survived at Paris [figure 64] signed by a Milanese armourer with the letters N. I.

In spite of the increasing technical skill of the German armourers, this second Italian fashion seems to have held its own in western Europe. For instance, Flemish paintings of the early sixteenth century almost invariably show very nearly flat breasts with a slight central keel, large shield-shaped tassets and armets of the Italian fashion.

A large number of good quality armours were being produced at this period for light troops, both horse and foot. These consisted of a light open-faced helmet, a gorget, a cuirass with knee-length, laminated tassets to strap round the leg, and a pair of light arms sometimes with gauntlets attached. The light horse armours were not all fitted with a

61 (*above*) The armour of the Elector Otto Heinrich, Count Palatine of the Rhine, attributed to Koloman Helmschmied, *c.* 1520

62 (*opposite*) Baron Thyssen's *Knight in a Lansdcape*, by Vittore Carpaccio, showing an armour of the Venetian fashion *c.* 1520; the squire wears the helmet

63 (*above*) Design by Jörg Sorg for the decoration of an armour for the German Joust by the armourer Conrad Richter of Augsburg, dated 1550; the targe is probably in the Real Armería, Madrid

lance rest and some had a close-helmet in place of the open-faced helmet. They vary in quality, the best being produced in quantity even by first class armourers.

In Italy fluted armours were out of fashion by *c.* 1520 but continued to be popular in Germany for another decade or more. Decoration at this period usually consisted of bands of rather scratchy etching with a hatched ground. The metal was first covered with a protective coat through which the design was scratched with a fine point. The plate was then treated with acid so that the scratched designs were permanently fixed on the metal. This style with a hatched background went out of fashion in Germany in the 1520s but remained popular in England until the third quarter of the century, and in Italy and France for much longer. The decoration was frequently gilt and a few armours, such as that of Galiot de Genouilhac in New York, were gilt all over. The *pointillé* and engraved decoration of the fifteenth century was also still in use. A magnificent example of this is the Silver Armour of Henry VIII of England, complete with its horse armour, engraved by Paul van Vreland between 1514 and 1519, and now in the Tower of London.

Typical of the sixteenth-century love of display are the armours imitating the puffed and slashed costume of the day. The portrait of Guidobaldo della Rovere by Angelo Bronzino (*c.* 1531–2) shows a restrained example in the Italian manner. The more exuberant slashed rolls of German costume were imitated with great vigour on an armour made by Koloman Helmschmied of Augsburg, son of Lorenz, about 1510 [figure 68]. The etching includes imitation of damask or cut velvet. The visor, illustrating another typical, early sixteenth-century feature, is embossed to represent the face of a man with aquiline nose and a long moustache. Similar visors, and others embossed in the form of animal masks, occur on many contemporary helmets. At first sight, the Helmschmied armour mentioned above appears to be intended purely for parade, but both in New York and in Dresden are its pieces of exchange to convert it for the field and tournament. A few armours of this period were decorated with pierced silver or brass plates sometimes backed with coloured cloth. The edge bands of some German armours were still decorated in the technique called *Goldschmelz* in which the design appears in gold on a ground of shiny blue oxide.

Koloman Helmschmied, working for the young Emperor Charles V, produced a garniture known as the 'K.D.' armour,

47

64 A Milanese armour in the Italian style of c. 1510–15, made by an armourer signing with the letters N. I.

one armour of which is largely in the Flemish fashion described above, [figure   ], and this is certainly one of the earliest garnitures made in the mature style of the sixteenth century. The etched decoration and the rows of embossed billets are confined to the edge bands of the principal pieces, a little embossing is found on the shoulders, couters and the standing guard of the left shoulder, while the remainder is left smooth and bright. The etched and gilt bands of this armour differ from the earlier type in that the ground of the design is eaten away, leaving the design itself slightly in relief. This was achieved by painting the decoration onto the metal and etching away the background, which is usually, but not always, decorated with many small dots. This style remained in use in Germany throughout the century. A professional etcher was employed on this work, thus an armour made for Charles V by Desiderius Helmschmied is signed and dated 1536 by the armourer's brother-in-law, Daniel Hopfer, better known for his prints. The painter Jörg Sorg also married into the Helmschmied family, and is particularly important since he kept a book of pen and wash drawings recording the designs he used on some forty-five armours between 1548 and 1563 [figure 63]. On most of them he recorded the date and the names of the patron and the armourer. This book is of great importance in identifying the work of Augsburg armourers, and a number of the pieces illustrated have survived, including an almost complete garniture made by Mathias Frauenpreiss in 1549 and 1550 for the future Emperor Maximilian II. However, as Sorg himself did not hesitate to use the same designs for different armourers, it is difficult, unless the plate is marked, to identify the work of an individual who belonged to a closely knit body of armourers, many of whom were related or had worked in each other's shops as apprentices. By this time, since the decoration in the bands was often partially embossed, cooperation between armourer and etcher must have been close. The bands now spread across all the broader plains of the armour and, a little later, floral scrolls were used freely all over the surface as in the work of Anton Peffenhauser of Augsburg [figure 86].

The K. D. armour, as well as having an armet, is already equipped with a burgonet, an open-faced helmet with a brim over the eyes. The face of this can be closed with a removable buff. A close-helmet turning on the gorget is also supplied, and many pieces of exchange. In armours made in the late 1520s, the armet is generally, though not invariably, re-

65 (*right*) Portrait by Titian of the future Philip II of Spain in parts of the 'Flower' garniture; a south German armour of *c.* 1550, much of which is still in the Real Armería, Madrid

66 (*below*) Part of the 'K.D.' garniture made for the young Emperor Charles V by Koloman Helmschmied, now in the Real Armería, Madrid

50

68 Parade armour of Frederick of Saxony, Grand Master of the Teutonic Order, made by Koloman Helmschmied of Augsburg before 1510

placed by a close-helmet with gorget plates attached to its lower edge overlapping the gorget of the armour. At first, the close-helmets had no comb, or a very low one, but the comb began to grow as the century progressed, reaching a considerable height c. 1590 and then once more decreasing. Late sixteenth-century close-helmets had much less prominent visors than formerly and a more vertical front profile.

In Germany c. 1530 the breastplate began to develop a central vertical keel and to project more prominently in the centre, as on the armour of Landgrave Philip I of Hesse which is dated 1534 [figure 69]. This armour is represented on the Landgrave's tomb but with its full pauldrons. The style of etching and the one-piece tassets suggest that this armour is an early product of a centre which provided armour for a number of other northern German courts, Brandenburg, Saxony and Brunswick. The armours, apparently made for the celebrations following the marriage of Julius, Duke of Brunswick and Lüneburg to Hedwig of Brandenburg in 1560, show the full development of the breast projection into a sharp point.

At the same time, in other German courts where Italian influence was stronger, the breastplate became flatter and longer waisted, until c. 1580, when again under Italian influence, the peascod breastplate was widely adopted in Germany. This fashion had first appeared in Italy about 1570, when the waistline became sharply pointed downwards at the centre and was overhung by a hump-like projection of the breastplate [figure 86]. The increasing size of the contemporary trunk-hose caused the tassets to become wider and wider at the hips in order to accommodate them. By the 1530s, some armours were fitted with long laminated tassets with poleyns attached to the end of them, as on the 'Firesteel Armour' of the Emperor Charles V at Madrid, the last work of Koloman Helmschmied, dated 1531, the year before his death. Finger gauntlets became popular once more. The laminated skirt of the backplate gradually became shorter until by the middle of the century it consisted of a single lame or even a mere flange made in one with the backplate.

The *Adlergarnitur*, so called because its decoration includes the eagle of Old Austria, made in 1547 by Jörg Seusenhofer of Innsbruck, for the Archduke Ferdinand II, magnificently displays the German style of the mid-century. This is one of the largest recorded garnitures and is provided with pieces of exchange and reinforces for use as a field

51

69 The armour of Philip I, Landgrave of Hesse, dated 1534, made by an unidentified German armourer

70 Part of the 'Burgundy Cross' garniture made by Wolfgang Grosschedel of Landshut for the future Philip II of Spain, in 1551

armour, as four different sorts of light armour for foot and light horse combat, as two different armours for foot combat within barriers and as four different suits for mounted combat in the lists [figure 72].

Probably the greatest of the Nuremberg armourers of this period was Kunz Lochner the Younger (c. 1510–1567). His garniture for Duke Johann Friedrich II von Gotha, and the two splendid horse armours in the Wartburg were lost in the Second World War, but a very similar horse armour apparently bearing his mark, is at Madrid, and the armour made by him for the Emperor Maximilian II is at Vienna. He also produced armour decorated with strapwork of coloured enamels on an etched ground [figure 77]. An armour of this type made for Sigismund II August of Poland, c. 1555, is at Stockholm.

The style of Wolfgang Grosschedel of Landshut (active c. 1515–1563) is very similar to that of the Helmschmied family. His most famous works are probably the 'Burgundy Cross' and the *de ondas ó de nubes* garnitures made for Philip II of Spain in 1551 and 1554 respectively, both of which the king is believed to have taken with him to England for his marriage with Mary Tudor [figure 70]. Grosschedel may have been one of the armourers brought over by Henry VIII when he founded his own royal workshop at Greenwich in 1515. Greenwich armour developed parallel to that of Italy, but certain particularly distinctive features can be seen throughout the period of production: except in a few early armours the wings of the couters are invariably made separately from the cap covering the point of the elbow, the pauldrons (which are large and give the armour a rather humped appearance) are constructed of narrow, overlapping lames and until the last quarter of the century have removable standing guards on either side of the neck, the profile of the upper bevor – the lower part of the visor – is concave, and the use of the close-helmet rotating on the gorget continued right down to the seventeeenth century after it had been abandoned elsewhere.

A number of armours made for the king himself have survived [figure 71] but the finest of the early products of the Greenwich shop is an armour dated 1527, traditionally belonging to Galiot de Genouilhac (1465–1546), *Grand Maître de l'Artillerie* and *Grand Écuyer du Roi* to Francis I of France. This armour is etched and gilt all over with foliage enclosing putti, monsters, merfolk, animals and the Labours of Hercules. The design and the etching are in the

71 (right) Portions of a Greenwich armour for the field and tilt of Henry VIII of England, 1540; part of the decoration is based on a design by Hans Holbein the Younger

72 (below) One of the foot-combat armours from the *Adlergarnitur*, made in 1547 for Archduke Ferdinand II of Austria by Jorg Seusenhofer of Innsbruck and etched by Hans Perckhammer

73 The future King Charles I, wearing what is apparently his late brother's Greenwich armour made by William Pickering, c. 1610

Italian manner and may have been carried out by the Florentine Giovanni da Maiano.

As at Augsburg, a pen and wash album has survived recording many of the armours, with the names of their owners, made by the Greenwich workshop in the second half of the century. A number of these armours are still in existence; others are known from portraits [figures 73 and 88]. The similarity of the designs of the Album armours and those used at Augsburg may be explained if, as it is thought, the master armourer for most of this period, Jacob Halder, was a native of that city. The suit made by Halder's successor, William Pickering (1605–18) for Henry, Prince of Wales, is at Windsor Castle. It retains its extra pieces for the tilt, and a portrait of Henry's brother, later Charles I, apparently shows the same armour with long tassets to the knee, which have not survived [figure 73].

Italy continued to produce armours for the field and tournament throughout this century, but there was a steady falling off in the quality of the decoration. The rather scratchy style was still commonly used, but by mid-century the German style was coming into use and by the third quarter of the century German designs were also fashionable. No great garnitures of Italian manufacture, similar to those made in Germany, have survived, but garnitures of more modest dimension were produced. The breastplate tended to grow longer from about 1530, becoming peascod about 1570. Laminated tassets are normal, of rather square outline and with many lames for foot combat, and shield-shaped and of three to five lames for mounted combat. Latterly, tassets for foot are made in one piece with the lamination simulated by embossing. The large German type couter was popular in Italy from the early years of the century, becoming smaller as the century progressed. Both kinds of couter now usually encircled the inside of the joint completely. For foot combat a small kettle-hat with a hazel-nut shaped skull and a slight flat brim, known as a Spanish morion was provided. Many armours are equipped with a comb morion, a form of kettle-hat with a high comb running fore and aft and with a brim turned up before and behind in sharp points [figure 85].

The best known of the armourers working in this style is Pompeo della Chiesa of Milan (active c. 1570 to c. 1600). The etched decoration is usually confined to bands divided by plain areas while the motifs frequently consist of trophies of arms and pieces of armour, bright on a dotted ground

74 Portions of a garniture made *c.* 1550 for Duke Johann Friedrich II of Gotha by Kunz Lochner of Nuremberg

either black or gold [figure 78]. In the case of an armour of a member of the Borromeo family of about 1580−85, the bands are broad with only half-inch bright bands between them, and the decoration consists of bands of strapwork deriving from German sources alternating with the bands of trophies which also contain the numerous badges of the owner.

75 Shield dated 1541 of the Emperor Charles V by Giacomo Filippo and Francesco Negroli

76 Cuirass in the antique style made by Bartolommeo Campi of Pesaro, c. 1540, probably for Guidibaldo II of Urbino

Italy is, however, much more famous for embossed rather than for etched armour. Many fifteenth-century paintings and statues show embossed armour in imitation of classical models but none of that date appears to have survived, although there is no reason to suppose that it did not exist. The armour of Donatello's St George, formerly on the Or San Michele at Florence, shows the influence of contemporary armour and could certainly have been worn. A complete armour in the antique style, made by Bartolommeo Campi of Pesaro in 1546, has survived at Madrid and the cuirass of another is in the Bargello at Florence [figure 76]. It was more usual, however, for embossed decoration of the late Renaissance type, satyr masks, scrolled foliage, mythical animals, cornucopias and so on, to be applied to armours of more conventional form. The metal was usually coloured blue or russet and decorated with gold and, occasionally, silver damascening. By far the most artistically successful of armourers working in this style was Giacomo Filippo Negroli, who was active 1531–1561. Quite apart from his remarkable technical skill in the handling of steel, his sense of design must put him in the first rank of Italian sculptors of his age. The shield of Charles V at Madrid, signed

77 Portions of a garniture decorated with coloured enamel made by Kunz Lochner of Nuremberg for Prince Nikolaus IV, the Black, Radziwill, c. 1555

78 Boot-stirrups from a garniture by Pompeo della Chiesa of Milan, late sixteenth-century; the decoration of the edge bands shows German influence

79 Part of the garniture *de los mascarones* (grotesque masks) of the Emperor Charles V by Giacomo Filippo and Francesco Negroli of Milan, 1539

80 (*right*) Parade armour of Eric XIV of Sweden, made by Eliseus Libaerts of Antwerp in 1563, and later purchased for the Elector Christian II of Saxony

81 (*below*) Part of an embossed armour of Philip II of Spain made by Desiderius Helmschmied and decorated by Jörg Sigman in Augsburg in 1548

PHILIPP. IACOBI · ET · F · NEGROLI · FACIEBANT · MDXXXXI illustrates the crispness of his embossing and the great delicacy of his damascened foliage scrolls, only surpassed by those of a shield at Vienna, also of this Emperor, unsigned but almost certainly by the same hand [figure 75].

The armour made by the Negroli family was not intended solely for parade. The garniture *de los mascarones* at Madrid made for Charles V in 1539 covers two pages of the *Inventario Illuminado*, the picture inventory of the Emperor's armour. It consists of two cuirasses, one made to look like an anime, or laminated cuirass, but in fact solid, a reinforcing breastplate, a kettle-hat, a burgonet with skull-reinforces and two visors to convert it into a close-helmet, a pair of legs and several pairs of arms and pauldrons. The embossing, which is very restrained but of the utmost crispness, is confined to the pauldrons, couters, poleyns and the skull of the burgonet. In the last place it can be covered by the skull-reinforce. Not only is the workmanship of the embossing and damascening of the very first order but the construction is so precise that it is quite difficult to see the joints of the lames [figure 79].

A second group of Italian embossed armours exists in which the whole surface is covered with putti, figures in

classical dress, animal masks amid swags of fruit and strapwork. The surface is usually further enriched by silver and gold damascening. The style, which lacks the restraint of the Negroli family and their command of the material, is attributed to the hand of Lucio Piccinino of Milan, on the strength of an armour at Vienna of Alessandro Farnese, Duke of Parma, for whom Piccinino is known to have produced a matchlessly beautiful armour [figure 83].

Examples of German embossing are known from the last quarter of the fifteenth century, but for the first half of the sixteenth century, embossed decoration, except on the costume armours mentioned above, is usually rather simple with bold designs and is confined mainly to the wings of couters and poleyns, spreading later to the tassets and pauldrons [figure 72], and the lowest lame of the tonlet when this is present. However, about 1548 Desiderius Helmschmied employed a goldsmith, Jörg Sigman (c. 1527–1601), to assist him in decorating an armour for Philip, Duke of Milan, later Philip II of Spain. This armour, which was completed in 1552, still survives at Madrid with its shield and saddle, while a second helmet is in New York. The decoration of grotesques amid strapwork and bunches of fruit with a few larger figures on the helmets, couters and the shield, is believed to be based on designs by the Spanish painter Diego de Arroyo. The work is inferior to the best Milanese work of the period [figure 81]. Anton Peffenhauser of Augsburg also produced an embossed armour of similar type for a king of Portugal, possibly employing the same embosser. It also survives at Madrid [figure 67].

The Augsburg armourers failed to break the Italian monopoly in embossed decoration, but as late as 1599 an armour was made in Augsburg decorated all over with low relief embossing, and with applied pierced and embossed gilt copper plates illustrating equestrian combats amid complex scrolling foliage. It was purchased in 1602 for the Elector Christian II of Saxony and is now in the Historisches Museum, Dresden [figure 82].

An important group of embossed armours exists, many of which bear badges and monograms associated with the court of France and particularly with Henri II. The embossing consists of masks, strapwork, grotesque and human figures in the Mannerist style, all in rather low relief. In almost all cases the designs are based on drawings by Étienne Delaune. Motifs used in the decoration of the palace of Fontainebleau also occur. It is thought that these must be

82 Parade armour, embossed and with gilt copper applied plaques, purchased from Augsburg for the Elector Christian II of Saxony, dated 1599

83 (*above*) Helmet of Alessandro Farnese, Duke of Parma, *c.* 1578, attributed to Luccio Piccinino of Milan

84 Portions of an armour for the field and tilt of George Clifford, third Earl of Cumberland, made at Greenwich, *c.* 1580–90

the products of a French Royal Armoury [figure 85]. A second very similar group occurs, apparently in some cases based on the same designs. One of these was bought for Eric XIV of Sweden from Eliseus Libaerts, a goldsmith of Antwerp in 1562. A second armour ordered in 1563 was captured by the Danes *en route* and is believed to be the one sold to Christian II of Saxony in 1606 by Heinrich Knopf

85 Gold and enamel morion and shield of Charles IX of France, made by Pierre Reddon, goldsmith of Paris, in 1572

86 Portions of a garniture made by Anton Peffenhauser before 1591 for the Elector Christian I of Saxony

of Nuremberg [figure 80]. A group of armours very similar in construction to those of Italy but with all-over decoration often of diagonal bars or closely set quatrefoils, of which a number, some associated with the Royal House, have survived in Paris, is believed also to be French. The armourers of Italy appear to have made and decorated armour to appeal to this taste.

The brigandine remained popular, its shape following contemporary civilian fashion. A number have survived at Madrid complete with arm defences of brigandine or splints and in one case with trunk hose of brigandine. The Titian portrait of Giovanni Francesco Aquaviva, Duke of Atri at Kassel, painted in 1552, shows a brigandine of red velvet and gilt nails with trunk hose and burgonet decorated *en suite*.

Even in this century the armour was not invariably worn uncovered. Heraldic tabards are frequently shown in English and Flemish sources of the first half of the century, and the *Inventario Illuminado* includes a large number of harness coats. Horse armour of plate was usually made *en suite* with the great garnitures, but many bards were of plain steel and were re-covered in rich fabrics for each festival or pageant. During this century heraldic crests were not worn in the field, their place being taken by bunches of ostrich feathers dyed in bright colours, but the crest did still find a place in the tournament. Three small wooden crests of this period have survived at Dresden.

Although the shield had completely gone out of use in central Europe for mounted combat, the buckler, the small hand shield, remained in use for fencing throughout this century. George Silver (1599) describes them as having a spike of about a foot long used for offence or for sword breaking, and he states regretfully that they were going out of fashion. Italian garnitures and a few German ones include a larger, round, steel shield decorated *en suite* with the armour.

ARMOUR BECOMES OBSOLETE

THE FIRST IMPORTANT BATTLE won by the use of hand firearms was Bicocca in 1522. From that event dates the decline in the use of armour in the field. The increasing efficiency of firearms made it impossible to make armour proof in every part, and mobility, the alternative form of defence, was impossible to achieve in ponderous armour.

Throughout the sixteenth century there was an increasing interest in the science of war and numerous books were written on tactics and the organization of armies. From these we learn of the different types of troops employed and the arms and armour thought suitable for each service. The *Battle of Alexandria* painted by Albrecht Altdorfer in 1529 shows the cavalry divided into fully armoured knights on barded horses and light horse in bands more or less uniformly dressed and armed. Derricke's *Image of Ireland*, 1581, shows the English army more or less uniformly armed, the heavy horse and pike in half-armours with plate arms, the light horse in mail shirts, and all wearing open comb-caps which were the only armour provided for the caliver men. The comb-cap was a kettle-hat with a comb running fore and aft over the skull.

By the end of the century armour had to be made so heavy, in an attempt to make it proof against musket shot, that writers, such as La Noue, stated that it was impossible to bear its weight for any length of time. At a Muster in 1590 when the troops refused to wear their armour on the march, the constables and the owners of the armour had to arrange for it to be carried in carts or in sacks on horseback; not only a shameful thing to do but exceedingly bad for the armour. Commanders were constantly recording their difficulty in making their troops wear their armour, and additional pay sometimes had to be granted to encourage them to do so. In 1607 De Gheyn illustrates the pikemen of the Guard of Prince Maurice of Nassau in cuirass, tassets and pot, but without arm defences. His caliver men have pots only and his musketeers no armour at all.

The heavy cavalry of von Wallhausen in 1616 wear three-quarter armours with close-helmets, full arms, a rein-

87 Prince Maurice of Orange by Michiel van Miereveldt, showing the armour presented to him by the States General after the Battle of Nieuwpoort (1600)

88 (*opposite*) Anonymous portrait of Henry Hastings, third Earl of Huntingdon, dated 1588, showing a Greenwich armour

89 Prince Tommaso of Savoy by Anthony van Dyck, painted in 1634

forcing plate to go over the breastplate, and boots in place of greaves and sabatons. This is the typical armour of the heavy horse of the Thirty Years War, and in the British Civil War of the 1640s two Parliamentarian regiments, Hazelrigg's Horse and the Earl of Essex's Guard were armoured in this way. Von Wallhausen's light horse are harqubuziers armoured only in an open casque and breastplate with cross-straps across the back. Robert Ward in 1639, describing such troops, states that their coat should be of buff leather. He also mentions companies of dragoons, mounted infantry consisting of pikes and muskets. By the middle of the century, the heavy cavalryman was rarely armoured in more than a pot, buff coat, cuirass and an elbow gauntlet on the bridle hand.

Writing in about the year 1670, Sir James Turner says, 'when we see Batallions of Pikes, we see them every where naked, unless it be in the Netherlands, where some, and but some Companies represent the ancient Militia; and we find an Universal defect in the Cavalry, as to the heavy armed, there being but few Cuirassiers in many Armies, and in very many none of them at all to be seen.' In fact, the cuirassier survived in European armies until the twentieth century

90 The future King Charles II aged fourteen, by William Dobson, in 1644; he is wearing an armour, probably of French make, which is still in the Armouries of the Tower of London

and serves to link the wearing of armour by airmen today with the knight of the Middle Ages.

In the seventeenth century the peascod cuirass was almost immediately replaced by a much flatter one of broader and shorter form. The tassets, whether the square ones for foot or the longer laminated ones of the cavalry, were now usually attached direct to the flange at the bottom of the breast. The close-helmet, usually of great weight, was now much more upright in profile and had broad gorget lames. The visor was frequently replaced by a grille of vertical bars or with a mask-like plate pierced over the eyes and mouth, both attached to a movable peak. The pauldrons, now that the lance was given up, were made symmetrical, usually with large square wings spreading over the cuirass. The arms were now riveted permanently to the pauldrons.

The burgonet was still popular for the light horse, but from about 1620 the most popular helmet for the cavalry was an open-faced one derived from Turkish examples. Examples of about 1551, illustrated in the etching book of Jörg Sorg, have high, pointed skulls in direct imitation of the Turks, but by the seventeenth century rounded skulls were more common. The neck was guarded by a laminated

91 An armour probably of a Prince of the House of Savoy, Milanese, *c.* 1600–10

92 Armour of James II, made by Richard Hoden of London in 1686

93 Field armour in the style of the Low Countries, made in 1619 by Jacob Topf of Innsbruck for the Archduke Leopold V

tail and the ears by flaps tied under the chin. Continental examples have adjustable nasals pierced through the peak and English examples usually have a face guard of bars attached to a movable peak [figure 92].

A few good quality armours were still being produced at different centres, the armourers of Greenwich in particular maintaining their high standard, but in general the finish was poor and all feeling for form disappeared. A full armour made for the young Prince of Wales about 1640 is in the Tower of London Armouries, and as late as 1668, a *cap à pied* armour made by Francesco da Garbagnate of Brescia was presented to Louis XIV by the Republic of Venice. The decoration of the armours of this period is usually by punching or engraving. Commanders continued to be painted in full armours long after it was in fact universally given up. In some cases the suits used can be recognised as historic armours and the issue to painters of armours from the Tower of London is frequently recorded.

The tournament was given up slowly during this century, its place being taken by riding at the ring and Turk's head. The cavalry spectacle known as the Carousel included these sports and occasionally a *mêlée*. In Copenhagen the actual quintains, moor's head and light lances used as late as the eighteenth century are preserved. Probably the most splendid of the carousels was that held by the young Louis XIV in 1662. The contestants, colourfully and splendidly disguised as Indians, Persians, Romans and 'Americans' are depicted in a special book prepared for the King with illustrations in gouache by Jacques Bailly.

THE SWORD AND DAGGER

THE HISTORY OF THE SWORD begins well over three thousand years ago, but it was only just before the opening of the period we are considering here that Scandinavian smiths began to make blades of steel. The Viking sword, with its broad blade designed mainly for hacking but pointed enough for a lethal thrust, was carried across Europe by the raiders, displacing the earlier blades designed only for cutting. The hilts of those swords had a short, cross-shaped guard above the hand and a heavy, laterally elongated pommel at the end of the tang to help balance the weight of the blade. Many of the better quality hilts were inlaid with silver or gold. The majority of blades were two-edged, about thirty-three inches long, with a deep groove down the centre to reduce the weight without weakening the blade. These swords are described in the Sagas and many have been excavated, not only from the graves of their owners but on battle sites or in fords. We know that they were greatly treasured, handed down from generation to generation, and considered as worthy gifts to kings and great warriors. The Middle Ages inherited not only the sword type but the veneration for the weapon. It became the symbol of justice and knighthood. Many were named, such as Roland's Durandel, and numerous blades have their maker's name inlaid in them, such as a sword at Reading signed by Ulfberht, apparently a Frankish smith.

The Bayeux Tapestry and other documents of that period show swords similar to those of the Vikings but with long

94 A chiselled steel hilt of c. 1670, possibly of French workmanship

95 (*left*) Rapier with gold and enamel hilt (at Vienna) given to the Archduke Ferdinand of Tyrol in 1554; the hilt is Spanish work of *c.* 1550

96 (*right*) The Coronation Sword of the French Kings, probably of twelfth-century date, but possibly earlier, traditionally the sword of Charlemagne

straight quillons and pommels shaped like a tea-cosy or brazil nut [figure 96]. This type remained popular until the middle of the thirteenth century.

In the twelfth century disk-shaped pommels became common (perhaps under southern European influence), blades tended to be longer and more slender, and quillons were either straight or curved up towards the blade. Brass, inlaid inscriptions, often of a religious nature, became popular, perhaps as a result of the Crusades. Inscriptions and even maker's marks are occasionally shown in the illuminations of manuscripts. By the end of the century the disk-pommel developed a hub-like protuberance on either face. This type, known as the wheel-pommel, remained in use throughout the Middle Ages. Although the quillons of fighting swords are usually of steel, the pommel was sometimes of jasper or rock crystal [figures 100 and 114].

Although very little is known about the art of defence as practised at this time, and it is thought that fencing consisted mainly of swapping blows and either catching them on the shield or stepping clear of them, there were already masters of arms plying their trade. A Statute of the City of London of 1286 forbids the keeping of schools, or teaching the art of fence within the City. On the mainland of Europe however, the masters of arms formed themselves into guilds, such as the Fraternity of St Mark in Frankfurt-on-Main which became the arbiters in everything to do with fencing in the German lands and the training centre for swordsmen. Until the end of the sixteenth century, masters did not confine themselves only to the sword but also taught two-handed sword play, the use of staff weapons and, as a last resort, wrestling. A number of most attractively illustrated *Fechtbücher* have survived, and the *Weisskunig* shows the young Emperor at practice with his fencing master.

The development of plate armour probably accounts for the introduction, at the beginning of the fourteenth century, of swords designed more specifically for thrusting, and for the appearance, a little earlier, of large cutting swords with longer grips intended to be used occasionally with both

98 Sword, early fourteenth-century, found in the Thames at Westminster; the locket bears the badge and slogan of the owner

99 The sword of tenure of Battle Abbey in Sussex made during the abbacy of Thomas de Lodelowe, 1417–34

hands. The latter appear to be described in contemporary inventories as *swords of war*. The blades of thrusting swords were usually tapered from the hilt to a sharp point and were of diamond section without a groove. Quillons were frequently turned sharply up towards the blade at the ends, and on swords with longer grips the pommel was usually pear- or kite-shaped, or of some other elongated form, in order to balance the increased length of the blade.

In southern Europe particularly, the sword was very frequently held with the forefinger over the quillon. This led, *c*. 1360, to the adoption of the *ricasso*, the edge of the blade, for some inch and a half from the hilt, being made blunt to avoid cutting the finger. About 1400, a small branch was sometimes made on the upper side of the quillon, curving round to protect the forefinger which passed through it. Later in the century a second curved branch appeared on the other side of the blade. Until recently these branches have been called the *pas d'âne* but Mr C. Blair has shown that this is incorrect and that they should be called the arms of the hilt. The swords of the Iberian Peninsula frequently show strong Moorish influence; the wedge-shaped quillons are curved up around the arms of the hilt, the flat disk pommel remained popular and decoration is often in the Moorish taste.

In Italy, in the latter part of the century, the lightly

100 (*right*) The sword and sheath of the Elector Friedrich the Warlike of Saxony, *c*. 1425; the pommel is of crystal, the sheath enriched with enamel

101 The Ceremonial Sword of Duke Christopher of Bavaria, probably German, c. 1480

102 (below) Sword, probably of Philip the Fair of Burgundy; Burgundian, c. 1490; the grip and pommel are of ivory

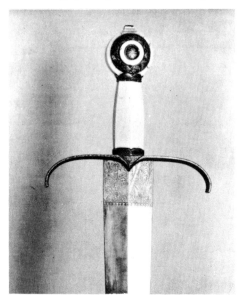

103 (right) The Ceremonial Sword of the Emperor Friedrich II, used at his Coronation by Pope Gregory IX in 1220; the pommel was replaced c. 1335 by the Emperor Karl IV

104 Sword with chiselled steel hilt by Othmar Wetter, dated 1594; a short blade springs from the pommel

105 (*right*) Sword of the Emperor Maximilian I by Hans Sumersperger of Hall in Tyrol, 1496

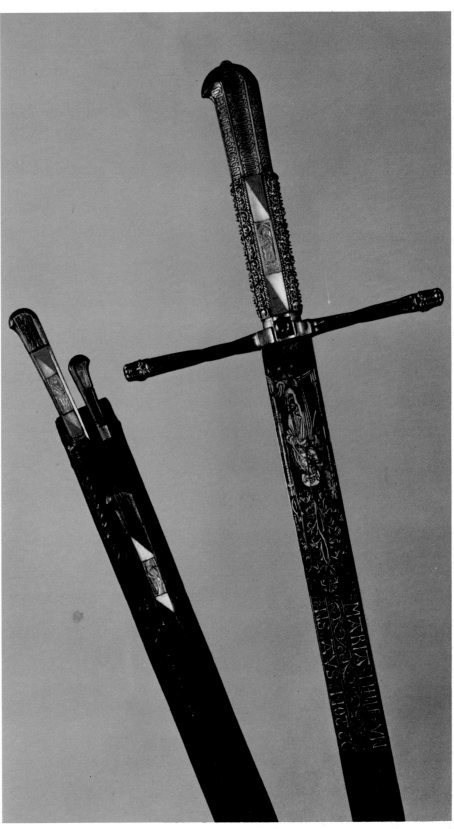

armed infantry, who wore no gauntlet, began to have swords with hilts designed to give greater protection to the hand: one quillon was bent up to form a knuckle-guard, the ends of the arms of the hilt were linked, and a ring was placed on the side of the quillons. For instance, the paintings of Lucca Signorelli in the monastery of Monte Oliveto Maggiore, c. 1497–1501, show swords of this type. After 1500, as the wearing of the sword with civilian dress became more usual and the duel more popular as a way of settling disagreements, more complicated guards developed. The majority of surviving mediaeval swords are severely plain, relying for their beauty on the excellence of their proportions. Highly decorated swords were, however, made and survive in the Treasuries of Europe [figures 100 and 101].

The design book of Filippo Orso, in the Victoria and Albert Museum, which is dated 1554, shows the complicated hilts of the period as well as simpler ones which were still the most popular for the full armoured man. These sketches indicate that all the guards found on hilts of the later sixteenth century were already in use. Additional rings sprang from the top of the arms of the hilt outside the hand, a Y-shaped guard linked the knuckle-guard to the same point inside, while the knuckle-guard itself often branched to join the larger of the rings outside the hand. While the hilts designed by Orso are rather cramped in their proportions, the portrait of the future Emperor Maximilian II by Antonio Mor at the Prado, dated 1550, shows a sword with thin, elegant guards and long, straight quillons. The sword of the Archduke Ferdinand of Tyrol is a fine example of the fully developed sword of the mid-sixteenth century [figure 95]. The hilt of enamelled gold is the work of an unidentified Spanish goldsmith of the first rank. Swords of the period, fitted with long, thin blades principally designed for thrusting, were known as rapiers. Their popularity seems to be due to the dominance of Spanish fashions. Ovoid pommels were now more or less universal, except in a few isolated groups of swords, such as those used in Dalmatia, where a square pommel was popular, and in Saxony where conical or pear-shaped pommels were fashionable.

According to George Silver, writing in 1599, '. . . the

108 English basket-hilted sword, *c.* 1610, the hilt encrusted with silver; traditionally of Sir William Twysden of Royden Hall, Kent

Italian teachers will say that an Englishman cannot thrust straight with a sword, because the hilt will not suffer him to put the fore-finger over the Crosse, nor to put the thumbe upon the blade, nor to hold the pummel in the hand, whereby we are of necessitie to hold fast the handle in the hand: by reason whereof we are driven to thrust both compasse and short, whereas with the Rapier they can thrust both straight and much further than we can with the Sword . . .'

Particularly in Saxony there was a tendency for the sword to have a rather short hilt with long spatulate quillons, a few small ring-guards and no knuckle-bow.

The system of fence that developed in the sixteenth century required many of the parries to be made with a dagger held in the left hand. These smaller weapons were made *en suite* with the rapier or sword. The use of dagger and sword together was first taught by Achille Marozzo of Bologna in his *Opera Nova*, 1536, but throughout the century the left hand was widely used for parrying or grasping an opponent's blade, and the cloak wrapped round the left hand remained in use much longer.

The late sixteenth century saw the development of more complicated guards, particularly by the addition of pierced shells on each side of the quillons. These became increasingly necessary as more stress was laid, in the books on fencing, on the use of the point, beginning with Camillo Agrippa of Milan writing in 1553. During the greater part of the century the leading school of fence appears to have been that of Bologna, but towards the end the Spanish school became fashionable. Captain Bobadil, in Ben Johnson's *Every Man in his Humour*, praises extravagantly the the Spanish master Jeronimo de Carranza, and even George Silver admits the popularity of this school.

Until the sixteenth century the decoration of the hilt usually consisted of plating and engraving, but in the sixteenth and seventeenth centuries the steel of the hilt was often chiselled in high relief with decoration which included all the motifs of contemporary taste. The Orso designs show hilts in the Mannerist taste which he states can be carried out in steel or silver, and many of the engravers who produced books of design at this time included a few for swords. The designs of Pierre Woeiriot of Lyon, *c.* 1550–60, show hilts almost entirely constructed of nudes, strapwork and grotesques, and the engravings of Virgil Solis also include a few of hilts and mounts decorated with his thin, interlacing strapwork and Mauresques. The mounts of swords,

109 The sword of King Sancho IV of Castile and León, c. 1290; the blade bears an etched inscription

daggers, sheaths, belts and purses might all be decorated *en suite*.

The only group systematically studied so far, is the Bavarian court school of which a number of steel chisellers are known by name and their work identified. The earliest of this group was Othmar Wetter who worked at Munich from 1583–89, and then moved to Dresden where he introduced his new style, displacing the rather fussy, over-decorated work of the Torgau smiths. The hilt signed by Wetter and dated 1594, now at Copenhagen, illustrates his style with its characteristic, deeply under-cut figures in niches [figure 104]. His mastery of steel chiselling is demonstrated by the precision and detail with which he rendered the human form in this intractable material. He was followed at Munich by the brothers Emanuel and Daniel Sadeler. Their style has nothing in common with Wetter's identified work. They decorated hilts, scabbard and purse mounts, firearms and powder flasks with characterstic designs in relief on a gilt ground based on the engravings of Etienne Delaune [figure 110]. A dagger hilt in the British Museum, by one of the Sadelers, is based on an engraved design for a pendant by Hans Collaert.

The hilt of the sword of the Spanish General Ambrogio di Spinola (1569–1630) is signed 'M.I.F.', which may indicate that it was made by Mathieu Jacquet, appointed *sculpteur et valet du chambre du roi* to Henri IV of France in 1597. This hilt, and another dated 1590 attributed to the same hand, are of steel chiselled in fine relief with New Testament scenes.

While chiselled steel hilts of varying quality are not uncommon, only a few of the gold and enamelled hilts worn by the very great have survived. It is clear from the study of portraits that they were never common. A gold and enamel hilt decorated in typical Augsburg fashion survives at Rosenborg. It was made for Christian IV of Denmark by Corvinianus Saur who was appointed court goldsmith in 1613. He had previously worked for the Bavarian court and published a series of designs for goldsmith's work in the 1590s. His work was not confined to weapons and a number of pendants by him are in existence. English hilts of the late sixteenth century and early seventeenth century are often decorated with rather characteristic, silver encrusting and very fine, gold damascening [figure 108].

The seventeenth century saw France become the leader of fashion and in consequence the French School of fence

110 Rapier, the hilt chiselled by Daniel Sadeler at Munich, first quarter of the seventeenth-century

became dominant under such masters as the Sieur de Liancour. The system was very much simplified and a lighter, more manageable sword with a shorter blade was used. The typical, early seventeenth-century civilian sword had short quillons and sometimes a slight shell guard. Complicated guards were no longer so necessary since the fencing system had become more efficient. Fine quality hilts were encrusted or damascened with silver or gold or more usually chiselled in high relief, like a rather later sword

81

111 Sabre with chiselled steel hilt in the Mannerist style, Italian, c. 1560; the blade is damascened with gold

112 Sabre with hand-and-a-half grip, Swiss or German, c. 1530

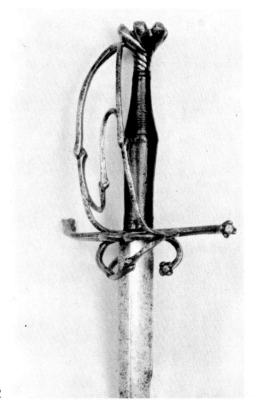

signed by Gottfried Leygebe of Nuremberg in the Victoria and Albert Museum.

By the end of the century the small-sword, the typical aristocratic weapon of the eighteenth century, was already fully developed. Its guard consisted of the arms of the hilt, already going out of use, a shell on each side of the hilt, a knuckle-guard now fixed to the pommel, and a small rear quillon. A heavier version of this hilt with scroll-guards flanking the knuckle-bow was popular in north-western Europe on cutting blades, and many silver-hilted examples lightly decorated with acanthus foliage exist.

In the seventeenth century, Spain, and Naples under Spanish influence, stood aside from the general line of development, continuing to use the long-bladed rapier and left-hand dagger. The characteristic hilt had long, thin, straight quillons, a thin knuckle-bow and a cup-shaped guard above the hand. Decoration was provided by piercing and chiselling the steel in very low relief, or, in late examples, by fine, low embossing.

The sword used in the tournament, a few examples of which survive at Madrid, had a plain cross hilt and both the point and edges were blunted. In the fifteenth-century foot-combat in the barriers, a two-handed thrusting sword was sometimes used with circular guards in front of each hand.

Single-edged swords have been found in Viking graves but, with the exception of broad-bladed falchions common in the fourteenth century [figures 26 and 37], were unusual until the introduction of curved swords at the end of the fifteenth century, apparently under eastern European influence. Many Italian parade swords with heavily decorated hilts in the Mannerist style have curved blades, animal headed pommels and simple S-shaped quillons [figure 111]. In Switzerland particularly there was a fashion for long, curved swords, often fitted with a hand-and-a-half hilt and complicated guards [figure 112]. Many German hand-and-a-half swords of the late fifteenth and early sixteenth centuries have long, straight, single-edged blades. One group of these are frequently described as hunting swords, but contemporary illustrations do not bear this out and they are to be seen in the hands of soldiers [figure 105]. Unlike the normal sword, where the grip is hollow and slips over the tang where it is secured by the pommel, the grip on these swords consists of two plates riveted to the sides of the flat tang. A number of this type have a small shellguard outside the hand.

In northern Europe the cutting sword retained its popu-

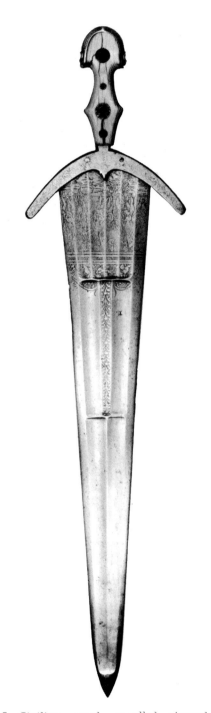

larity. Relatively short, broad-bladed swords with quillons curved into a figure of eight were the typical weapons of the Landsknechts [figure 62]. Later in the century additional guards were developed almost entirely enclosing the hand. From these derive the typical basket-hilted cavalry weapons of northern Europe throughout most of the seventeenth and eighteenth centuries [figure 108].

The long *sword of war* of the fourteenth century became increasingly popular in northern Europe during the fifteenth, reaching very large proportions in the following century. It was used both as a weapon for the strongest men told off to guard the colours, and for ceremonial purposes as it still is today. Northern two-handed swords were designed almost entirely for cutting. The blade can be shortened in use by grasping it with the hand before the quillons. Many examples have a leather cover to this part of the blade and hooked lugs to act as subsidiary quillons when the hand is in this position. The two-handed sword occurs only occasionally in Italy: those in the Arsenal at Venice are made with a sharp, reinforced point for thrusting. Throughout the sixteenth century, the art of fighting with the two-handed sword was still taught by the leading masters of arms.

The names of rather more blade smiths than hilt makers are known, since the former more often signed their work. The chief sword-making centres in the Middle Ages seem to have been Cologne, Passau and later Solingen in the north, and Milan, Brescia and Toledo in the south. Bundles of blades were exported from these centres all over Europe to be mounted on arrival in the fashion of the country.

Until the fifteenth century, blades were not usually decorated, unless inlaid inscriptions, makers' marks, and religious or cabalistic signs can be considered as decoration, but the sword of Sancho IV of Castile and León (*d.* 1295) bears an etched inscription [figure 109]. From the late fifteenth century etched decoration becomes common on blades of good quality. Hunting swords of the sixteenth century sometimes have scenes of the chase etched all down the blade. A group of blades of the second quarter of the century are signed by Ambrosius Gemlich of Munich who also etched an armour made by Wolfgang Grosschedel for Konrad von Bemelberg which is now at Vienna. The blades made by Clemens Horn of Solingen for the English court in the early years of the seventeenth century are etched with laudatory inscriptions and coats of arms all richly gilt. Some Italian parade swords have blades decorated with gold damascening.

113 Civilian sword, so-called *cinquedea*, Italian, *c.*1490; the etching is in a style reminiscent of Ercole dei Fideli of Ferrara

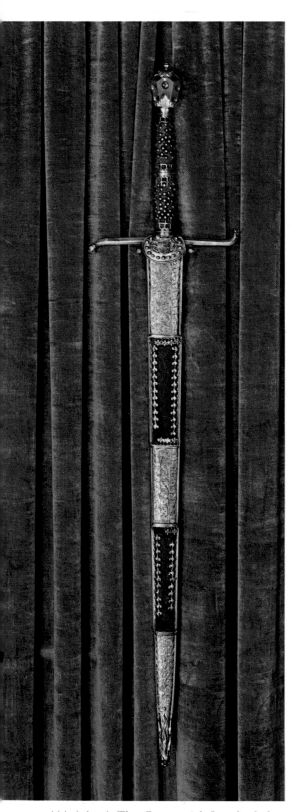

Numerous types of short swords or large daggers were used by both civilians and military throughout the whole period. Many are merely small versions of the normal sword, others have special forms of their own. One of the most popular from the late fourteenth to the end of the sixteenth century, known apparently as a *baselard*, probably because it came originally from Basle, had a handle like a capital I. It seems to have spread across most of Europe but survived longest in Switzerland.

Designs exist for sixteenth-century daggers of this type with richly decorated mounts and sheaths by such artists as Hans Holbein (1497/8–1543) and Heinrich Aldergraver (1502–*c.* 1555). Many have sheaths decorated with pierced

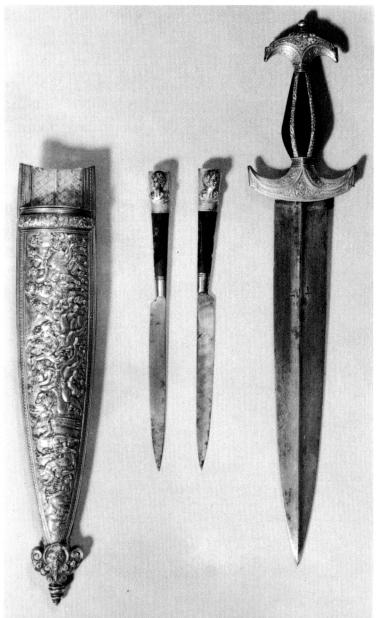

114 (*above*) The Ceremonial Sword of the Dukes of Franconia, *c.* 1460

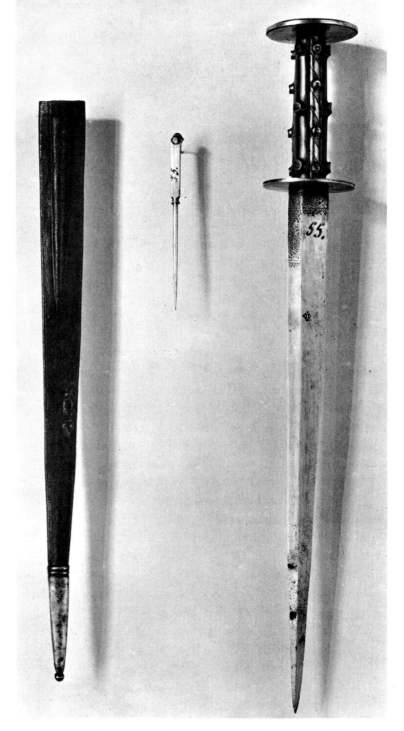

115 (*right*) Rondel dagger with sheath and brog, probably of Philip the Fair of Burgundy; Spanish, *c.* 1490–1500

116 (*left*) Dagger, dated 1585, probably made by the Basel goldsmith Jeremias Faesch. The two small knives fit into the front of the sheath which is decorated with the story of the Prodigal Son

gilt metal after Holbein's *Dance of Death* or with scenes from the legend of William Tell [figure 116].

In Italy there was a fashion, in the fifteenth century, for very broad-bladed short swords or large daggers usually ivory hilted and with fine, etched blades, some of which have been attributed to Ercole dei Fideli, a goldsmith of Ferrara [figure 113].

117 Dagger with steel hilt chiselled with Old Testament scenes; north Italian, mid sixteenth-century

During the fifteenth century one favourite form of dagger, known today as a rondel dagger, had circular or octagonal guards above and below the hand. The blade was usually of triangular section but more suitable for stabbing than cutting [figure 115]. One form of dagger which was in use from the early fourteenth century until the seventeenth, and latterly was particularly favoured in Scotland or north England, had a handle of somewhat phallic form.

Although effigies and paintings show that mediaeval daggers were sometimes made *en suite* with the sword, the *Fechtbücher* and the description of combats, such as those of Jacques de Lalain, show that they were not intended to be used together. The dagger was used when the sword was broken or lost, or to give the *coup de grace* to a defeated foe. Throughout the Middle Ages the dagger was normally used with the point projecting below the hand, but during the sixteenth and seventeenth centuries, when used in conjunction with the sword or rapier, it was held point upwards.

At the beginning of the period under discussion, the sword was at first normally worn on a belt encircling the hips and was later hung on straps from a waist-belt. However, in the thirteenth century the sword is quite often shown worn on a shoulder-belt by both soldiers and civilians, as in the Nine Heroes Tapestries in New York, and this method was again adopted in the late seventeenth century. Towards the end of the fifteenth century, the sword was usually hung on two straps from the waist-belt with a third diagonal strap to prevent it swinging wildly. The Portinari altarpiece and one or two other sources show the scabbard tied down to the thigh in the way that the American gunmen at a later date tied down their revolver holsters.

The scabbard consisted of two strips of wood shaped to fit the two sides of the blade and enclosed in a tightly fitting cover of leather, fabric or in some cases metal. Until about 1300 the scabbard was laced to the belt, thereafter it was usually attached by means of rings fixed to metal mounts on the scabbard. The mount at the mouth and any other mounts for suspension rings were called the lockets and the metal guard at the point was called the chape. In the seventeenth century and later, scabbards were often made of unlined leather, with only a chape and a hook to fit through a frog on the shoulder-belt.

OTHER WEAPONS

118 'Christ taken captive' from *The Large Passion* of Albrecht Dürer, 1510, showing a variety of infantry weapons

THE SIMPLEST, AND ONE of the earliest of human weapons, is the spear, basically no more than a sharpened stick. In the tenth and eleventh centuries the infantry spear was usually fitted with a long-bladed head with lugs on each side of the socket. This type went out of general use by the thirteenth century but is probably the ancestor of the spear used for boar hunting at a later date, which had a broad, leaf-shaped blade and either fixed lugs or a cross-bar to prevent the weapon sinking too far into this exceptionally dangerous prey. Also, probably descended from this kind of spear, is a whole family of weapons with long, broad blades, sharp on both edges and often with curved lugs at the base of the blade, like the partizans still carried by the Yeomen of the Guard. Mediaeval terminology is very imprecise and in many cases it is not possible to equate the names found in inventories or chronicles with actual surviving weapons. The 'thre grayned staves' may be a variety in which the subsidiary flukes are straight and are set at an acute angle to the blade [figure 119]. The *corseque* is another variety, while the word *langdebeve* probably refers to a similar spear but without lugs.

From the thirteenth century, the commoner form of infantry spear, later known as the pike, had a small, diamond-shaped head on a long staff, usually made of ash wood. It was a favourite weapon of the Swiss who developed special tactics to exploit it both as a defence against cavalry and as an offensive weapon for a charge in column. Its use was copied by the Germans in the Landsknecht Regiments, and by the French and eventually by all Europe. It was the decisive weapon in many battles of the fifteenth century, but its use by the Scots, without supporting halberdiers, against the archers and billmen of England at Flodden in 1513 indicates its limitations. The improvement of hand firearms was eventually to drive the pike from the field, but throughout the sixteenth and seventeenth centuries regiments were formed partly of pikes and partly of shot, the former serving to keep the cavalry at a respectful distance from the latter. The pikemen formed three or four deep and, with their weapons thrust forward through their own ranks, formed an impenetrable hedge. Towards the end of its life the pike

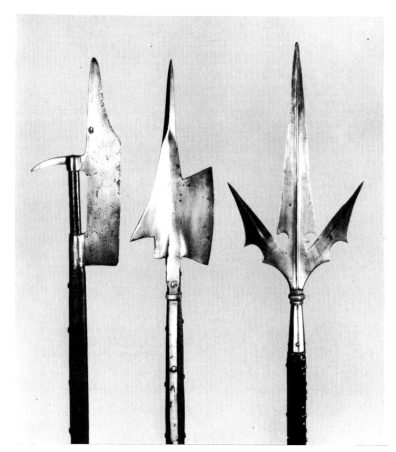

119 Three infantry staff weapons: halberds of the early and late fifteenth century, and what is possibly a 'thre grayned' staff

120 (*opposite*) Left to right: partizan of the guard of Louis XIV of France, *c*. 1670–80; glaive of the guard of Cardinal Scipione Borghese, *c*. 1620; halberd of the guard of Archduke Ernst, Governor of the Low Countries, 1593

reached its extreme length, varying between sixteen and twenty-two feet. The head was attached to the shaft by long steel straps to prevent them from being lopped off by the cavalry. The grip, called the *arming*, was of leather or velvet, to prevent the hand from slipping when wet with sweat or rain. Randle Holme (1682) mentions the socket, 'an Iron or brass hoop set on the foot of the pike to secure it from bruising'. The pike survived until the early eighteenth century as an infantry weapon, but already in 1670, Sir James Turner was writing in his *Pallas Armata* that the pike, 'the Prince of Weapons', was falling into disuse. Its place was eventually taken by the bayonet.

Early cavalry spears were probably identical to the second type of infantry spear, described above, but by 1300 they were already being made with rather longer and more slender points. Shortly after this, special lances with three or more small points were adopted for jousting. These were usually fitted with a hand-guard called a vamplate and a form of stop, called a graper, to prevent the couched spear from being forced back under the arm. From the end of the fourteenth century, this stop, now found also on war spears,

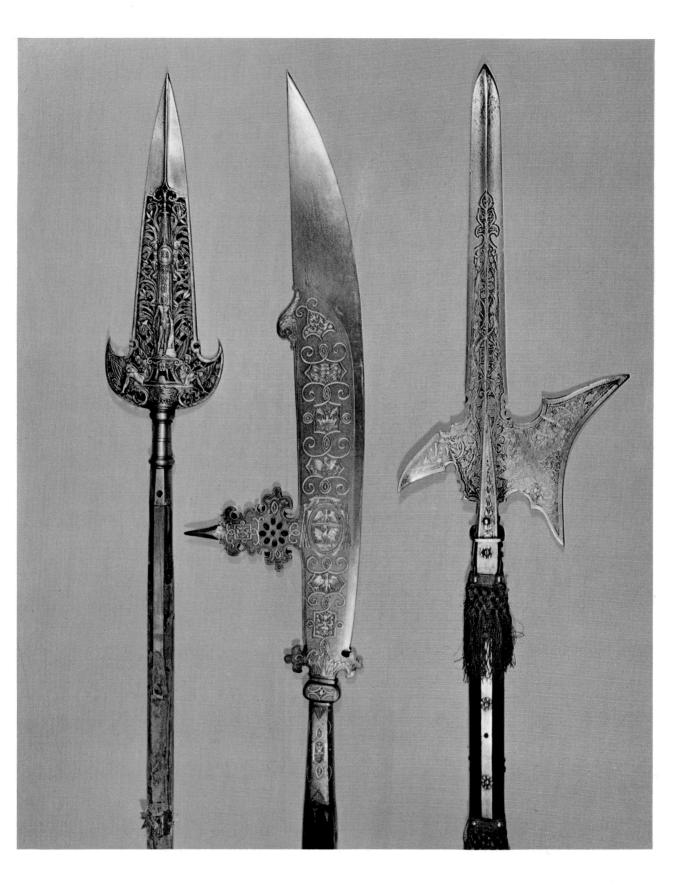

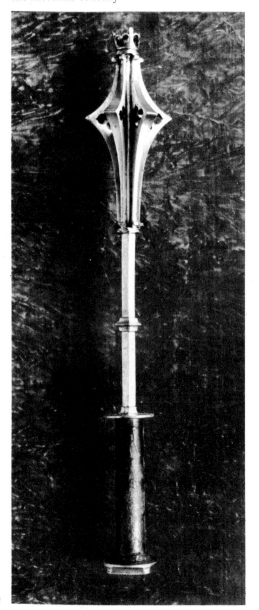

121 Mace, probably German, second half of the fifteenth-century

fitted against a bracket on the breastplate called an *arrest* or lance-rest. From the fifteenth century onwards, the heavy spear or lance for joust or battle was made thicker before and behind the grip. The lighter lance was, however, retained for the lightly armed horse, such as those of England, of Spain and of the march lands of eastern Europe. Particularly in Spain the light lance was frequently thrown like a javelin. Early in the seventeenth century the lance went out of favour in western Europe, to be reintroduced by Marshal Saxe in the middle of the eighteenth century.

The dart was a light, throwing spear, often fitted with flights and a broad barbed head like a gigantic arrow. It was particularly popular in Spain and Ireland.

The club was probably man's earliest weapon, and its derivative, the mace, has always been a popular weapon. Since the twelfth century, when maces with flanged metal heads are known to have been used, there was no basic change, although the shape of the flanges altered with the progress of taste. The development of plate armour and the difficulty of piercing it with a sword, made the mace increasingly popular. It became the typical weapon of the Sovereign's Sergeants-at-Arms and thus achieved a symbolic significance second only to the sword. The maces of Sergeants-at-Arms were clearly sometimes purely symbolic even in the fourteenth century when enamelled ones are recorded. Fifteenth-century maces tend to be light and elegant in keeping with the feeling of the period [figure 121]. They are usually decorated with architectural motifs, sometimes, as in an example at Vienna, of great richness. Renaissance examples are more robust, often with the edges of the flanges heavily scrolled. The finer examples are often damascened in gold and silver. The weapon retained its popularity until the eighteenth century in eastern Europe. Maces or spiked clubs with long shafts remained typical weapons of the poorly armed infantry until the seventeenth century.

The war hammer was used by both cavalry and infantry. The former carried a short shafted, light weapon with a long, very sharp, rear spike [figures 27 and 124]. Like the mace, it changed very little throughout the whole period except in decoration. Again, it was particularly useful against plate. The infantry maul was a heavier weapon with a shaft between four and six feet long, often with a head of lead. It was probably one of those weapons with an agricultural background which Mons. C. Buttin considered de-

122 Axe and mace head, both probably early fourteenth-century, found in London

veloped as a result of the First Crusade when the actual peasantry went to war, taking whatever weapons lay to hand. On the land it would have been used for driving in stakes, and contemporary illustrations such as the Luttrell Psalter show it breaking clods on the fallow. A number of lighter hammers with long shafts and armour piercing flukes at the back of the head were used, such as the Lucerne hammer and the *bec-de-corbin*. The latter was particularly popular in the fifteenth century for combat in the barriers [figure 123].

Axes, like clubs, are very early weapons. The axe of Viking times, with its great curve-edged blade and four foot shaft, was adopted by the Saxons and remained popular throughout most of Europe until the sixteenth century. In the fifteenth century, as the polaxe, it was popular with knights fighting on foot. The back of the head was fitted with a hammer or flukes, and both ends of the shaft bore sharp steel spikes. A smaller version of the head fitted to a shorter shaft was frequently carried by mounted men to supplement the sword. These additional weapons, and sometimes a second sword, were hung on the saddle bow.

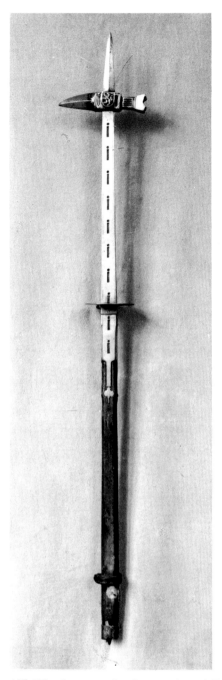

123 War hammer for foot-combat of Duke Sigmund of Bavaria, second half of the fifteenth century

124 (*opposite*) War hammer decorated with silver and gold overlay, south German, second half of the sixteenth century

Another important form of long-hafted axe was the halberd. First heard of in the thirteenth century as a Swiss weapon, it appears to have originated as a cleaver-like blade attached by two loops to a shaft seven or eight feet long. From the earliest times the top of the blade seems to have been pointed to form a thrusting weapon and before long a rearward spike was also attached to the top loop [figure 119]. It is to this weapon that the Swiss attribute their success against the Austrians at Sempach in 1386. In later examples the socket for the shaft is tubular, and from the fifteenth century narrow, steel straps extend downwards from the head guarding the sides of the shaft to which they are riveted. The head was now more axe-shaped and the top point often reinforced to pierce armour [figure 119]. These long, heavy weapons could deliver a blow of great force and the heaviest armour was not always proof against them. In the sixteenth century, halberdiers and pikemen were brigaded together to form the main body of the infantry of most European armies. In a more attenuated form the halberd remained in use from the early seventeenth century until the late eighteenth as the distinctive weapon of sergeants of Foot Regiments.

Late examples of all these weapons are found with etched and gilt decoration and were intended purely for display in the hands of bodyguards.

The principal missile weapon of the Middle Ages was the bow. It took two main forms, the simple bow and the crossbow. The ordinary bow, consisting of a piece of wood bent into an arc and held in tension by a cord joining the ends, was in use throughout Europe at the beginning of our period. The bow stave seems to have been about five feet long, but his early wars brought Edward I into contact with the longer and heavier elm bows of South Wales. This bow shot an arrow a clothyard long capable, as Giraldus Cambrensis tells us, of piercing an oak door four inches thick. In the hands of well trained and disciplined infantry deployed according to a new tactical theory, the bow gave England the ascendancy in her continental wars for a century.

Although archery was still encouraged by law in England throughout the reign of Henry VIII, himself a great bowman, its use steadily declined during the sixteenth century. Finally in 1595 the bow was forbidden to the forces of the crown by Order of Council. The yew bow, although so well known in legend and ballad, was at one time reserved by law for the best archers, and bows of other woods were more

common. Roger Ascham in his *Toxophilus*, 1545, gives careful instructions for choosing a bow of good long-grained wood preferably from the trunk of the tree, the wood of the branches having too many knots. 'If you come into a shoppe, and fynde a bowe that is small, long, heavy and strong, lying streyght, not windyng, not marred with knot, gaule, wynde-shake, wem, freate or pynche bye that bowe of my warrant.' Mediaeval illustrations frequently show the arrow passing on the right side of the bow, the opposite side to that used by modern archers. The extreme range of the long bow was over 400 yards; several of the marks on Finsbury Fields were at twenty-score yards and three were at twenty-one score. Ascham advises that the best sheaf arrows for war should have shafts of ash wood, and flights of goose feathers. The use of peacocks' feathers, such as those used by Chaucer's Yeomen, he clearly considered a vanity. The goose, he says, 'is mans comforte in war and in peace slepynge and wakynge'.

The head of the arrow was steel, at first fairly broad, but later examples designed to pierce plate armour, or find its joints, were more acutely pointed. Hunting arrows usually had broad-barbed heads so as to cause a fatal wound, and some had forked heads shaped like a Y. The arrows were either carried in a quiver worn on the hip, or simply thrust through a loop on the belt.

Ascham advocates the use of a bracer on the inside of the left wrist and a shooting glove on the right hand. 'A bracer serveth for two causes, one to save his arme from the strype of the strynge and his doublet from wearynge, and the other is, that the strynge glydynge sharpelye and quicklye of the bracer, may make the sharper shoote . . . A shootynge Glove is chieflye for to save a mannes fyngers from hurtynge, that he maye be able to beare the sharpe stryng to the uttermost of his strengthe.'

The crossbow consisted of a much shorter, stiffer bow fixed to a stock set at right angles to the bow. The cord was pulled back until it fitted behind a groove cut in the face of a revolving cylinder, called the nut, on the stock. It could be held thus in the spanned position without putting any strain on the arms. The arrow was placed on the stock in front of the bow string. A trigger underneath the stock was used to release the nut and discharge the bow. Early examples were spanned by hand. Throughout the Middle Ages lighter bows were spanned with a hook on the waist-belt which fitted over the string. The foot was placed in a stirrup

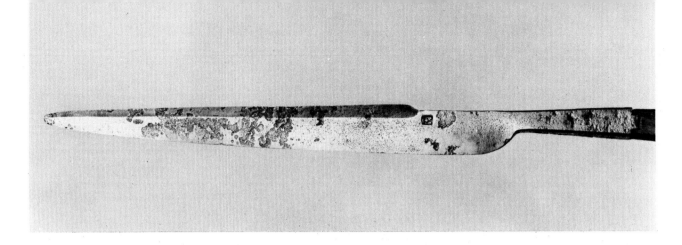

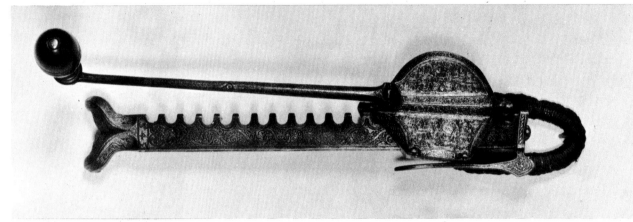

125 (*top*) A fifteenth-century glaive; the original staff would have been some four to five feet long

126 Rack for spanning a hunting crossbow, south German, dated 1545

on the front of the bow and pushed down to draw the bow [figure 7]. Later, various mechanical methods were devised for spanning, thus allowing the bow to be made stiffer and stronger. The heaviest war bows were spanned by means of a windlass and large hunting bows by a rack and pinion device which fitted onto the stock and was carried at the belt when not required [figure 126]. The range of the larger bows seems to have been much the same as that of the longbow. In the fourteenth and fifteenth centuries the majority of crossbows were composite, the bow being made up of laminations of horn. In the fifteenth century, steel bows became more popular, and, in the following century, replaced the early kind completely. The stock is usually more or less straight with a slight taper to the rear, but in the seventeenth century some German crossbows have a stock like that of the contemporary rifle. The wood was often inlaid or overlaid with pieces of carved or engraved bone or antler, and inlaid with pieces of engraved mother-of-pearl in exactly the same way as contemporary gun stocks. The crossbows sent to Spain by James VI and I in 1614 were inlaid with sheets of gold none of which unfortunately now survives in the bows at Madrid [figure 127]. Sixteenth-century bows were fitted with very complicated locks incorporating hair-triggers. Some had adjustable peep-sights.

The arrows shot from the crossbow, known as bolts or quarrels, were short and thick compared to those of the longbow. They were 'feathered' with thin wood or leather and a variety of heads were used, rather similar to those of the longbow arrow. The bolts were carried point upwards in a quiver at the waist, which fifteenth-century illustrations often show covered with stiff hair probably of badger or boar. Very occasionally the quiver also carried a large hunting knife as in the *Resurrection* by Hans Multscher, *c.* 1435, at Berlin-Dahlem.

The advantages of the crossbow were that it did not re-

127 (*below*) Crossbow, English, early seventeenth-century: part of the present sent by James I of England to Philip III of Spain in 1614; the gold inlay from the stock is missing

128 (*bottom*) Stone or pellet bow, Italian, *c.* 1580; it bears the arms of Wratislaus, Baron von Bernstein, Grand Chancellor of Bohemia

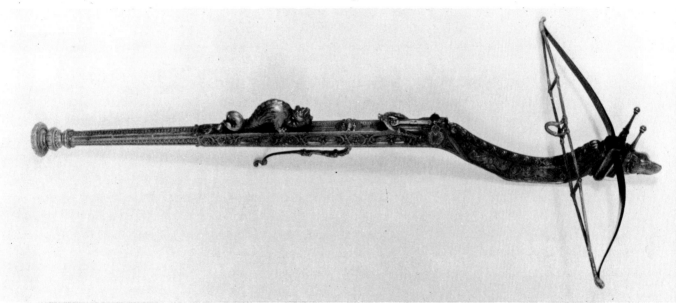

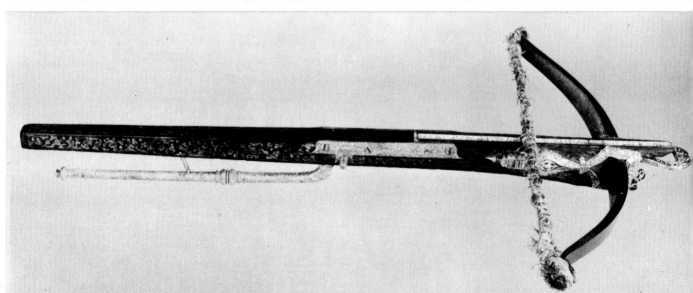

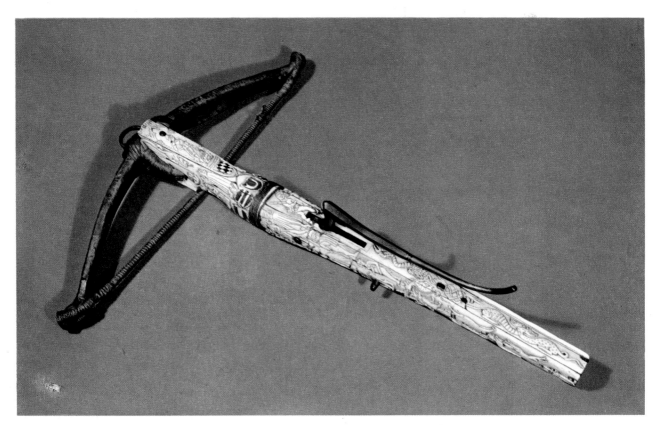

129 Crossbow, the stock overlaid with carved ivory, Bavarian, c. 1450–70; the bow of steel is covered with painted parchment

quire great strength to span it, nor was long training required to use it, and it could be held for long periods fully spanned without straining the arms. In the field it was often shot from behind a large shield, called a pavise, which gave the archer cover behind which to reload. For hunting, as compared with the arquebus, it was relatively silent and therefore did not alarm the game. The Electoral armoury at Dresden contains large numbers of these highly decorated bows, which were kept for use at the great deer drives for which the court was famous.

A light form of crossbow, with a double string for propelling stones or pellets, was very popular with both sexes from the sixteenth century onwards for shooting small birds and rabbits [figure 128]. The stone-bow of Queen Catherine de Medici has survived at Paris. It is not clear whether fourteenth-century references to stone-bows refer to this type or to a simple bow used for casting a stone, as no illustrations of the crossbow for stones has been noted earlier than the sixteenth century.